Contemporary's

WORD POWER

Spelling and Vocabulary in Context

Advanced 2

CONTEMPORARY BOOKS

a division of NTC/CONTEMPORARY PUBLISHING GROUP
Lincolnwood, Illinois USA

Acknowledgments

Series Developer
Phil LeFaivre
    Cottage Communications
    Sandwich, Massachusetts

Series Reviewer
Joan Loncich
    Instructor, Adult Basic Education
    Barnstable Community Schools
    Hyannis, Massachusetts

ISBN: 0-8092-0839-3

Published by Contemporary Books,
a division of NTC/Contemporary Publishing Group, Inc.,
4255 West Touhy Avenue,
Lincolnwood (Chicago), Illinois 60646-1975 U.S.A.

Credits

Market Development Manager
Noreen Lopez

Editorial Development Director
Cynthia Krejcsi

Project Manager
Laurie Duncan

Interior Design and Production
PiperStudiosInc

Cover Design
Kristy Sheldon

Word Power

Table of Contents

To the Teacher

Goals of the Series

Word Power provides the mature learner with a systematic program of instruction for reading, writing, and spelling the words needed on the job, at home, and in the community. The vocabulary is arranged thematically at appropriate levels of difficulty and presented in meaningful contexts.

Key Features

1. Word Power *provides instruction at five levels of difficulty, so that you can select the book that precisely fits your students' needs.*

   Each of the five *Word Power* books is keyed to a level of the *Tests of Adult Basic Education*, Forms 7 & 8. The *Introductory Level* correlates with Level L. *Word Power Intermediate 1* and *Intermediate 2* are tied to TABE levels E and M. *Word Power Advanced 1* and *Advanced 2* match levels D and A. The four upper-level books offer a pre-test to confirm appropriateness of level and to provide a comparison for post-test purposes.

2. *Words are presented in meaningful contexts. Students immediately see the importance of what they are studying and become motivated to complete the work successfully.*

   Units in the four upper-level books are keyed to one of six Comprehensive Adult Student Assessment System (CASAS) Life Skills Competencies: Consumer Economics, Health, Employment, Community Resources, Government and Law, and Learning to Learn.

3. *The skills of reading, writing, and spelling are synchronized to facilitate learning and build a portfolio of successful work.*

   Once students have analyzed the meaning and spelling of the words, they can apply what they have learned in a practical writing and proofreading exercise. Letters, announcements, or similar realistic messages that students write can be mailed or kept in a portfolio of each student's work.

4. *Regular review tests in standardized testing formats allow you to monitor progress while familiarizing your students with the testing strategies they will find in typical GED exams and tests of adult basic skills.*

   Every four-lesson unit concludes with a two-page review test. It checks each student's progress in mastering the meaning and spelling of the words. The testing formats match those used by the TABE.

5. *The easy-to-use format and a Mini-Dictionary at the four upper levels empower students to take control of their learning and work with a high degree of independence.*

   Each lesson follows a sequence through four key stages of learning, described on page 8. Students can work independently and progress at their own rate.

6. *The important* Introductory *book provides basic instruction in the key phonetic principles and mechanics skills in a meaningful adult context.*

   Unlike most programs for mature learners, *Word Power* provides instruction in the basic principles of sounds and letters, and it accomplishes this through high-interest, mature content.

Using the Advanced 2 Book

Like all the books in this series, *Advanced 2* consists of twenty-four lessons. After each unit of four lessons, a Review Test is provided to check progress. Each lesson is divided into four parts. Each part brings to closure a coherent step in the learning process. Depending on your students and your instructional time block, one or more parts or an entire lesson might constitute a class session.

The reading level in this book has been carefully controlled. It matches the reading level of TABE Level A.

The Pre-test on pages 10 and 11 will provide assistance in evaluating how much your students know and placing them in the appropriate *Word Power* text. No single test, however, should serve as the sole guide to placement. Used in conjunction with other tests of reading and writing, as well as your own observations, this Pre-test can serve as a valuable resource.

The lessons in this text include many related language skills not covered in the Pre-test. A better strategy might be to allow students who do well on the Pre-test to progress through the lessons independently at an accelerated pace.

The Post-test on pages 144 and 145 can serve as a handy tool for checking progress. Both tests cover selected words in this text, so a comparison of scores will provide a gauge of each student's progress.

In addition to the Pre-test and Post-test, each text includes a Personal Word List page and a How to Use the Dictionary page. The Personal Word List page allows students to record words encountered outside the classroom. These words can be studied using the steps in How to Study a Word on page 9. They can also be shared and discussed with the class as a means of enhancing each lesson. This is usually best done as part of the writing and proofreading part of the lesson.

The instructions for completing each part are clearly stated and could be performed by many students with a high degree of independence. You may prefer to have students check their own work using the Answer Key on pages 166 through 171. They can record the number correct in the space provided at the bottom of most pages.

As you can see, *Word Power* is an effective and practical tool for addressing the needs of a wide variety of adult learners. We feel confident that *Word Power* will make a significant contribution to your vital work as a teacher.

Breaking Down a Lesson

Each lesson in *Word Power* progresses through the following stages of instruction:

Ⓐ Check the Meaning

On these two pages, students read the words in the context of one or two essays related to the unit theme. Students are asked to infer the meanings of the words from the context and then choose the correct definitions in a multiple-choice format. These exercises, like most of the exercises in the lessons, lend themselves easily to both independent and cooperative learning.

Ⓑ Study the Spelling

This page contains a wide variety of exercises designed to focus attention on the letters and word parts that make up the spelling of each word. Emphasis is placed on noting coherent clusters of letters, tricky sound/letter combinations, and related and inflected forms of the words.

Ⓒ Build Your Skills

Using one or more of the list words as a springboard, this part focuses attention on important language skills, such as recognizing homophones, inflectional endings, prefixes, suffixes, capitalization, and punctuation. Practice activities follow a concise statement of the rule and examples.

Ⓓ Proofread and Write

The lessons conclude by having students apply what they have learned. First students proofread an example of writing related to the lesson theme. Then they correct the errors they find. This is followed by a structured writing assignment modeled on the format they have just proofread. Students proofread and correct their own work and make a final copy for their writing portfolios. Cooperative learning strategies can be employed by having students share a draft of their written work with a classmate and solicit his or her response before making the final copy.

How to Study a Word

Follow these steps for learning how to spell new words.

1 **Look**
at the word.

- How many syllables does it have?
- Do you know what the word means?

2 **Say**
the word aloud.

- What vowel sounds do you hear?
- What consonant sounds do you hear?

3 **Cover**
the word.

- Can you see the word in your mind?
- What are the sounds and letters in the word?

4 **Write**
the word.

- How is each sound spelled?
- Can you form the letters carefully?

5 **Check**
the spelling.

- Did you spell the word correctly?

6 If you make a mistake,
repeat the steps.

Pre-test

Part 1: Meaning

For each item below, fill in the letter next to the word or phrase that most nearly expresses the meaning of the first word.

> **Sample**
>
> hammer
>
> (A) part of the arm   (C) a type of vegetable
> ● a tool used for driving nails   (D) to mix thoroughly

1. proliferate
- (A) support
- (B) discuss
- (C) spread
- (D) plant

2. benevolent
- (A) generous
- (B) recipient
- (C) erratic
- (D) elderly

3. idyllic
- (A) smart
- (B) uneducated
- (C) clever and witty
- (D) simple and peaceful

4. homogeneous
- (A) cloudy
- (B) impure
- (C) alike
- (D) healthy

5. vie
- (A) compete
- (B) mix together
- (C) filthy
- (D) expand

6. adamant
- (A) relaxed
- (B) firm
- (C) excellent
- (D) wrinkled

7. emulate
- (A) burn
- (B) copy
- (C) sorry
- (D) cheerful

8. malady
- (A) music
- (B) wealthy
- (C) secret
- (D) illness

9. compulsory
- (A) complete
- (B) sudden
- (C) required
- (D) satisfactory

10. plausible
- (A) reasonable
- (B) restful
- (C) portable
- (D) quiet

GO ON ➡

Part 2: Spelling

For each item below, fill in the letter next to the correct spelling of the word.

11. (A) assess   (C) assese
    (B) asess   (D) ases

12. (A) vacine   (C) vaccine
    (B) vacksine   (D) vacene

13. (A) referal   (C) referril
    (B) referral   (D) refuril

14. (A) innoculate   (C) inaculate
    (B) inoculate   (D) inocilate

15. (A) dissension   (C) disension
    (B) disenssion   (D) dissenssion

16. (A) admitance   (C) admitttance
    (B) admitence   (D) admittence

17. (A) feasable   (C) feesible
    (B) feasible   (D) feazible

18. (A) sieze   (C) seize
    (B) seeze   (D) seise

19. (A) insidous   (C) insideous
    (B) incidious   (D) insidious

20. (A) discrepancy   (C) discripancy
    (B) discrepency   (D) descrepancy

21. (A) pertanent   (C) pertinant
    (B) pertinent   (D) pertenant

22. (A) colaboration   (C) callaberation
    (B) collaberation   (D) collaboration

23. (A) casualty   (C) caseulty
    (B) casuelty   (D) casualtey

24. (A) prolifrate   (C) proluferate
    (B) proliferate   (D) prolifurate

25. (A) accellerate   (C) accelarate
    (B) acelerate   (D) accelerate

26. (A) impertinent   (C) impertanent
    (B) impertinant   (D) impurtinent

27. (A) manuver   (C) maneuvar
    (B) manover   (D) maneuver

28. (A) prerequasit   (C) prerequisite
    (B) prerequizit   (D) preriquasite

29. (A) partisan   (C) partisen
    (B) partizan   (D) partasan

30. (A) valuminous   (C) voluminus
    (B) voluminous   (D) volumanus

STOP

Rules of the Road

Ⓐ Check the Meaning

Read the paragraphs below. Think about the meaning of the words in bold type.

The automobile is a source of both love and hate. We love the feeling of freedom it gives us as we **maneuver** through traffic or across the open highway. We hate it when there is no place to park or when we are stuck in traffic. Like it or not, knowing how to drive is almost a necessity today.

To drive legally, you must get a license. The process begins with a test on the traffic rules. Passing this test allows you to **procure** a learner's permit. The test asks what a driver should do in certain **circumstances**. For example, it may ask when a **pedestrian** has the right of way.

Once you have a learner's permit, you may drive an automobile if an experienced, licensed driver accompanies you. This **restriction** requires beginning drivers to learn from people with lots of driving experience. Start by driving slowly on little-used side streets. **Statistics** show that speed and inexperience are the cause of many accidents. Trying to do too much too soon might make you a **casualty**.

When you have mastered all the driving skills, you are ready for the final test. This test involves driving a **prescribed** course with an officer who evaluates your driving. Now you must **endeavor** to demonstrate how well you drive. This road test is usually conducted in a quiet and serious manner. It is not a time for idle conversation or **verbose** behavior. Listen carefully to the directions the officer gives you and perform them smoothly. Avoid **erratic** movements, and use your turn signals. Always maintain a reasonable speed.

Once you have earned the license to drive, you must continue to drive safely. A series of minor violations or one serious violation could cause you to **forfeit** your driving privileges.

Check the Meaning

Choose the correct meaning for the word in bold type. Fill in the circle next to the correct meaning.

1. To **procure** is to
- Ⓐ get.
- Ⓑ steal.
- Ⓒ create.
- Ⓓ destroy.

2. Another word for **maneuver** is
- Ⓐ mark.
- Ⓑ move.
- Ⓒ provide.
- Ⓓ guess.

3. A **statistic** is a
- Ⓐ form of electricity.
- Ⓑ type of computer.
- Ⓒ place to stand.
- Ⓓ fact expressed in numbers.

4. Another word for **circumstance** is
- Ⓐ circle.
- Ⓑ neighborhood.
- Ⓒ area.
- Ⓓ condition.

5. When people **forfeit** something, they
- Ⓐ fasten it to something else.
- Ⓑ give it up.
- Ⓒ pretend to love it.
- Ⓓ criticize it.

6. Another word for **verbose** is
- Ⓐ truthful.
- Ⓑ poisonous.
- Ⓒ wordy.
- Ⓓ polite.

7. A **pedestrian** is
- Ⓐ someone traveling on foot.
- Ⓑ part of a clock.
- Ⓒ a person dressed in an unusual way.
- Ⓓ a doctor who treats children.

8. Another word for **restriction** is
- Ⓐ responsibility.
- Ⓑ confusion.
- Ⓒ title.
- Ⓓ limitation.

9. A **casualty** is
- Ⓐ an informal way of dressing.
- Ⓑ someone killed or injured.
- Ⓒ a greeting.
- Ⓓ a high-speed highway.

10. If something is **prescribed**, it is
- Ⓐ prevented.
- Ⓑ lost or confused.
- Ⓒ directed or ordered.
- Ⓓ written.

11. To **endeavor** is to
- Ⓐ try.
- Ⓑ avoid.
- Ⓒ pull apart.
- Ⓐ show favor for.

12. An **erratic** movement is
- Ⓐ entertaining.
- Ⓑ unbelievable.
- Ⓒ misleading.
- Ⓓ unpredictable.

B Study the Spelling

Word List

statistic	restriction	forfeit	casualty	erratic	endeavor
verbose	procure	maneuver	circumstance	prescribed	pedestrian

Write the list word or words for each clue.

1. It is formed from the word *restrict*. _____

2. The word *cure* is part of its spelling. _____

3. They end with *tic*. _____ _____

4. It is formed from the word *prescribe*. _____

5. It begins like *circumvent* and ends like *distance*. _____

6. There is an *ei* in the spelling of this two-syllable word.

_____

7. The word *casual* is part of its spelling. _____

8. It has three syllables. The middle syllable is *neu*. _____

9. This word comes last in alphabetical order. _____

10. It begins like *endear* and ends like *favor*. _____

Write the words with four syllables. Circle the word that begins like *pedal*.

11. _____ **12.** _____

Add the missing syllable. Write a list word.

13. sta_____tic _____

14. _____cure _____

15. pre_____ _____

16. maneu_____ _____

17. er_____ic _____

18. for_____ _____

19. circum_____ _____

20. restric_____ _____

Score: ____ / 20

Ⓒ Build Your Skills

Language Tutor

A sentence is a group of words that express a complete thought. It begins with a capital letter and ends with a period, a question mark, or an exclamation point.

A *statement* ends with a period.   Always endeavor to do your best.

A *question* ends with a question mark.   Did you procure the supplies?

An *exclamation* ends with an exclamation point.   Don't hit that pedestrian!

Write these sentences. Add capital letters and end punctuation.

1. unless the team arrives soon, it will forfeit the game

_____

2. did the workers follow the prescribed steps

_____

3. what an erratic maneuver

_____

4. the candidate's verbose speech put me to sleep

_____

Use each group of words to write the type of sentence stated. Add capital letters and end punctuation.

5. Statement: a new restriction

_____

6. Exclamation: the latest casualty

_____

7. Question: dangerous circumstance

_____

8. Statement: a surprising statistic

_____

Score: / 8

Ⓓ Proofread and Write

Shana studied the booklet she received for her driver's license test. She copied the following sentences from the booklet to help her remember them. She made three spelling mistakes. She also made a mistake in capitalization and end punctuation. Cross out the misspelled words and the mistake in capitalization. Write the correct spellings above them. Add the correct punctuation.

Statistics show that drinking and driving cause most accidents.

Always stop for a pedestrien in a crosswalk.

Certain prescribed medicines affect your ability to drive. any restricktion should be labeled on the bottle.

How can you avoid being a highway casulty

• Never drive in an erratic manner.

• Endeavor to obey all rules.

• Be patient. Do not try to maneuver through heavy traffic at high speeds.

Writing Portfolio

On another piece of paper, write some of your own rules for driving. Use at least four list words. Be sure to use capital letters and end punctuation.

Proofread your rules carefully and correct any mistakes. Then make a clean copy and put it in your writing portfolio.

Borrowing Money

Ⓐ Check the Meaning

Read the paragraphs below. Think about the meaning of the words in bold type.

It sounds so easy: just sign on the line and you will have plenty of money to spend as you like. Then repay the loan in small, easy payments. It sounds like a **bargain** until you **analyze** the fine print. The payments may last for sixty months or more. You may end up paying twice the amount you borrowed.

Prudent borrowers shop around for a loan just as they do for anything else. Loans that are easy to obtain are always the most expensive. A credit card is this type of loan. Experienced shoppers **refrain** from using the credit card whenever possible. If they do use it, they pay the entire amount billed each month. This way interest costs can be avoided. The **novice**, however, is more easily **enticed** by the ability to spend all the money he or she likes. It is very easy to run up a large debt that takes years to repay.

Choose the correct meaning for the word in bold type. Fill in the circle next to the correct meaning.

1. A **prudent** borrower
   - Ⓐ is careless.
   - Ⓑ does not need much money.
   - Ⓒ owes many people money.
   - Ⓓ is careful and sensible.

2. A **novice** is
   - Ⓐ a beginner.
   - Ⓑ someone who works for a bank.
   - Ⓒ an expert on loans.
   - Ⓓ kind to others.

3. To **analyze** something is to
   - Ⓐ look into its history.
   - Ⓑ erase it.
   - Ⓒ put it to sleep.
   - Ⓓ examine it closely.

4. A **bargain** is
   - Ⓐ a building used for storing things.
   - Ⓑ something offered at a low price.
   - Ⓒ equipment used in a gymnasium.
   - Ⓓ a type of weapon.

5. When people **refrain** from something, they
   - Ⓐ keep it nearby.
   - Ⓑ bend it back.
   - Ⓒ hold back from doing it.
   - Ⓓ chill it.

6. Another word for **entice** is
   - Ⓐ deliver.
   - Ⓑ uncover.
   - Ⓒ tempt.
   - Ⓓ push.

Check the Meaning

Read the paragraphs below. Think about the meaning of the words in bold type.

Loans fall into two categories: secured loans and unsecured loans. A secured loan is taken for an **explicit** purpose, such as buying a car. The borrower must **surrender** that property to the lender if the loan is not repaid. A secured loan costs less because it **assures** the lender that the loan will be repaid. However, because a car decreases in value as it gets older, the lender will probably **insist** that the loan be repaid on a strict schedule. In addition, the lender will usually lend only part of the full price. This guarantees that the car is always worth more than the amount owed on the loan.

An unsecured loan relies on the borrower's promise to repay the money. When someone uses a credit card, he or she is taking an unsecured loan. These loans **pose** a higher risk to the lender, so the rates are higher. In some cases, the rates may even **fluctuate**. Credit cards may offer a low rate for the first six months. Then the rate may triple. This type of loan can end up being very costly.

Choose the correct meaning for the word in bold type. Fill in the circle next to the correct meaning.

7. To **insist** is to
  (A) deliver.
  (B) demand.
  (C) harm.
  (D) imagine.

8. An **explicit** purpose is
  (A) difficult to understand.
  (B) foolish.
  (C) unimportant.
  (D) clearly defined.

9. When people **pose** something, they
  (A) present it.
  (B) take a picture of it.
  (C) steal it.
  (D) misplace it.

10. To **surrender** something is to
  (A) divide it into parts.
  (B) stop it from happening.
  (C) rename it.
  (D) give it up.

11. To **assure** is to
  (A) surprise.
  (B) pretend to be helpful.
  (C) state with complete certainty.
  (D) delay for a long period of time.

12. If something **fluctuates**, it
  (A) glows.
  (B) changes.
  (C) glides through the air.
  (D) has a musical sound.

Score: / 12

B Study the Spelling

Word List

explicit	bargain	assure	prudent	insist	entice
pose	refrain	fluctuate	analyze	novice	surrender

Write the list word or words for each clue.

1. The word *gain* is part of its spelling. _____

2. It has three syllables and a double consonant in its spelling.

   _____

3. It has one syllable and four letters. _____

4. It is formed from the word *analysis*. _____

5. They end with *ice*. _____ _____

6. It has three syllables and ends with *ate*. _____

7. It has two syllables and a double consonant in its spelling.

   _____

8. It has two vowels. Both vowels are *i*'s. _____

Circle the list word within each of these words. Then write the list word.

9. insistence _____

10. explicitly _____

11. enticement _____

Form a list word by matching the beginning of a word in the first column with its ending in the second column. Write the list word.

pru	frain	12. _____
nov	dent	13. _____
fluc	lyze	14. _____
re	ice	15. _____
ana	tuate	16. _____

Ⓒ Build Your Skills

Language Tutor

A dictionary gives the pronunciation of each entry word. It uses special symbols that stand for the sounds. If a word has two or more syllables, the dictionary shows which syllable is stressed. The stressed syllable is in bold type and has a small mark over it.

Word	Pronunciation
pose	pōz
bargain	**bär´** gĭn
prudent	**proōd´** nt
explicit	ĭk **splĭs´** ĭt

Study the complete list of sounds and symbols on page 146.

Study each pronunciation. Write the word that matches the pronunciation.

1. ĭn **sĭst´**   insure   insist   interest   _____

2. **rā´** dē ō   raid   radical   radio   _____

3. **fĭng´** gər   finger   finish   final   _____

4. kôrt   court   kennel   core   _____

5. nīf   night   knife   knee   _____

6. **sĕn´** tər   center   sender   chapter   _____

7. ĭn **stôl´**   instill   install   instant   _____

8. soō **pîr´** ē ər   superior   somewhere   sincere   _____

9. **trĕzh´** ər   treaty   treason   treasure   _____

10. **flĕk´** sə bəl   flakes   flexible   fabulous   _____

11. hĭ **rō´** ĭk   heroic   hero   herring   _____

12. **līt´** nĭng   listening   littering   lightning   _____

13. **pŏz´** ĭ tĭv   possible   positive   possess   _____

14. kəm **păkt´**   compact   contact   compare   _____

15. lăm   lamb   lamp   land   _____

D Proofread and Write

June made a list of questions to ask when she applied for a car loan. She made four spelling mistakes. Cross out the misspelled words. Write the correct spellings above them.

Questions to Ask about My Car Loan

☐ Do you inist on checking my credit history?

☐ Who will anilyze my application and decide if I get the money?

☐ Is your interest rate as good as one from my credit union? Where can I get the best bargain?

☐ Can the interest you charge fluxuate in the next three years?

☐ If so, can you be explicit about how much it might change?

☐ Is it prudant to pay back the loan in thirty-six months?

☐ When can you assure me I will get the loan?

Make a list of questions you would ask when applying for a loan. Use at least four list words.

_____

_____

_____

_____

_____

Writing Portfolio

Proofread your list of questions carefully and correct any mistakes. Then make a clean copy and put it in your writing portfolio.

The Plastic Revolution

(A) Check the Meaning

Read the paragraphs below. Think about the meaning of the words in bold type.

Some people call it the plastic revolution. Others refer to it as the cashless **society**. No matter what it is called, the use of bank cards has caused some **fundamental** changes in how people handle money. How did the revolution come about? For years, most workers deposited their paychecks into checking accounts. Then they wrote checks to **retrieve** cash or to pay for purchases. In recent years, many employers decided it would be more **expedient** to put the money directly into each worker's checking account. This practice, called direct deposit, has reduced the **anxiety** many workers have about losing a check or getting to the bank too late. Instead of a paycheck, the employee gets a notice saying that the **transaction** has occurred. Computers take care of the rest.

Another important factor in the revolution is an **apparatus** called the automatic teller machine, or ATM. This machine can **dispense** cash from an account twenty-four hours a day. A bank card allows depositors to get this cash from their accounts. Users must enter a secret password to **thwart** anyone who tries to use a lost or stolen card. If the password **deviates** by a single letter, the ATM seizes the card.

Bank cards have changed the way people spend money. These cards can now be used to pay for purchases in retail stores and service stations. Unlike a credit card, a bank card is not a tool for borrowing money. Instead, a bank card moves money from a person's account into the account of the store. Each use **depletes** the amount of money in a person's account. People do not yet live in a cashless society. However, as the uses for bank cards **proliferate**, society moves closer to plastic and farther away from cash.

Check the Meaning

Choose the correct meaning for the word in bold type. Fill in the circle next to the correct meaning.

1. Another word for **anxiety** is
   - (A) happiness.
   - (B) pain.
   - (C) worry.
   - (D) embarrassment.

2. A **fundamental** change is one that is
   - (A) basic.
   - (B) unnecessary.
   - (C) humorous.
   - (D) a matter of life or death.

3. To **deplete** is to
   - (A) repeat.
   - (B) reduce.
   - (C) punish.
   - (D) wrinkle.

4. A **society** is a
   - (A) group of people with something in common.
   - (B) religion.
   - (C) slight pause in a speech.
   - (D) grand social event that takes place in the summer.

5. To **proliferate** is to
   - (A) earn money.
   - (B) shout aloud.
   - (C) divide in half.
   - (D) spread rapidly.

6. An **apparatus** is
   - (A) an opening in a wall.
   - (B) a device or machine.
   - (C) a type of decoration.
   - (D) a sharp blade.

7. To **dispense** is to
   - (A) throw into disorder.
   - (B) hold down.
   - (C) give out.
   - (D) destroy.

8. When people **deviate** from something, they
   - (A) lower its value.
   - (B) mark it clearly.
   - (C) copy it.
   - (D) move away from it.

9. If something is **expedient**, it
   - (A) costs a great amount of money.
   - (B) has no color.
   - (C) is suitable and practical.
   - (D) is dangerous.

10. To **thwart** is to
    - (A) injure.
    - (B) block.
    - (C) increase in size.
    - (D) plan ahead.

11. When people **retrieve** something, they
    - (A) get it back.
    - (B) raise it again.
    - (C) send it away.
    - (D) check it carefully.

12. A **transaction** is a
    - (A) way of moving heavy loads.
    - (B) business affair or action.
    - (C) path followed by a star.
    - (D) spiritual experience.

Score: / 12

B Study the Spelling

Word List

society	deviate	dispense	apparatus	fundamental	deplete
proliferate	retrieve	expedient	anxiety	transaction	thwart

Write the list word or words for each clue.

1. These two list words rhyme. _____ _____

2. It begins with three consonants. _____

3. There is a double consonant in its spelling. _____

4. The word *action* is part of its spelling. _____

5. It begins like *depend* and ends like *complete*. _____

6. They have an *ie* in their spelling. _____

_____ _____ _____

7. It has four syllables. The last syllable is *tal*. _____

8. It begins like *dispose* and ends like *license*. _____

9. The word *life* is part of its spelling. _____

10. It has three syllables. The middle syllable is *vi*. _____

Add the missing letters. Write the list word.

11. app___rat___s _____

12. prolif___r___te _____

13. disp___n___e _____

14. th___ ___rt _____

Write the list words that come between these words in the dictionary.

15. demand _____ _____ direction

16. steam _____ _____ type

17. example _____ _____ parade

18. razor _____ _____ tape

Score: ___ / 18

Ⓒ Build Your Skills

Language Tutor

A final *y* following a consonant is usually changed to *i* before adding an ending.

society + -es = societies   happy + -ness = happiness

A final *e* is usually dropped before adding an ending that begins with a vowel.

deviate + -ing = deviating   retrieve + -able = retrievable

Write each sentence. Follow the directions in parentheses to add the missing word.

1. The doctor soothed our (anxiety + -es) about the operation.

_____

2. That large meal certainly (deplete + -ed) our supply of food.

_____

3. All of us were impressed with her (friendly + -ness).

_____

4. The store has magazines on every (imagine + -able) topic.

_____

5. Ed is busy (arrange + -ing) the furniture.

_____

6. I like that (arrange + -ment) very much.

_____

7. The experience taught me a (value + -able) lesson.

_____

8. It rained (steady + -ly) for two days.

_____

Score: ⟋ 8

D Proofread and Write

Joan planned to visit her bank. She made a list of questions to ask about her new bank card. Joan made four spelling mistakes. Cross out the misspelled words. Write the correct spellings above them.

- Is there a charge for using the ATM to dispense just $20?

- If the ATM does not return my card, how do I retreive it?

- What is the fundamentel difference between a bank card and a credit card?

- Would it be expedient to replace my old credit cards with this bank card?

- I feel some anxiety about using the ATM. Is it a complicated aparatus?

- Only a few stores now accept a bank card. Do you expect the number of stores that accept the card to prolifirate in the next few years?

Make a list of questions you have about bank cards or any other banking service. Use at least four list words.

_____

_____

_____

_____

_____

 Writing Portfolio

Proofread your questions carefully and correct any mistakes. Then make a clean copy and put it in your writing portfolio.

Tenants and Landlords

Ⓐ Check the Meaning

Read the paragraphs below. Think about the meaning of the words in bold type.

A landlord and a tenant have a **mutual** interest in honoring the terms of a lease. If each respects the rights of the other, both benefit. The tenant's obligation does not end when the rent is paid. He or she must respect the landlord's property and be a good neighbor to tenants in **adjacent** apartments. Noise or **unsightly** piles of trash **degrade** an entire neighborhood. When residents quarrel over such problems, the landlord must **mediate** their differences.

The landlord's most important obligation is to maintain the property. Broken appliances, a leaky roof, or pest problems should be reported promptly in writing. If the landlord does not live in the building, he or she may be **oblivious** to the problems. A landlord is more likely to respond to the needs of a good tenant. A good tenant is as valuable as a good landlord.

Choose the correct meaning for the word in bold type. Fill in the circle next to the correct meaning.

1. Another word for **mutual** is
Ⓐ unusual.
Ⓑ ridiculous.
Ⓒ simple.
Ⓓ shared.

2. When people **mediate** a problem, they
Ⓐ work with two sides to get an agreement.
Ⓑ refer it to others for a solution.
Ⓒ refuse to get involved with it.
Ⓓ solve it through the use of medicine.

3. If two things are **adjacent**, they are
Ⓐ kept apart by a high fence.
Ⓑ side by side.
Ⓒ at war with each other.
Ⓓ on opposite sides of a lake.

4. When people **degrade** something, they
Ⓐ praise it.
Ⓑ lower its value.
Ⓒ delay it.
Ⓓ repair it.

5. Another word for **unsightly** is
Ⓐ blind.
Ⓑ immoral.
Ⓒ delicious.
Ⓓ ugly.

6. When people are **oblivious** to a problem, they
Ⓐ take it very seriously.
Ⓑ give it to another person.
Ⓒ are unaware of it.
Ⓓ solve it quickly.

Check the Meaning

Read the paragraphs below. Think about the meaning of the words in bold type.

Before signing anything, it is always wise to **scrutinize** the small print. Not all leases are alike. In some cities, **legislation** has defined additional rights and responsibilities for tenants and landlords. Most cities and towns make smoke detectors **compulsory** in all homes and apartments. It is the landlord's responsibility to install them. If heat is included in the rent, the landlord is required to maintain a certain **minimum** temperature. Any **violation** may be reported. In most areas, the law does not allow the heat to be cut off during winter for any reason.

Tenants, too, may have added obligations. Most renters must pay a deposit as well as the last month's rent. If the tenants **vacate** the apartment before the end of the lease, the landlord may keep the additional month's rent. The landlord may keep the deposit only if the apartment is left in poor condition. What the landlord expects should be clearly understood when the lease is signed.

Choose the correct meaning for the word in bold type. Fill in the circle next to the correct meaning.

7. If something is **compulsory**, it is
   - (A) full of holes.
   - (B) required.
   - (C) beautiful.
   - (D) hidden.

8. The **minimum** of anything is
   - (A) its highest part.
   - (B) a legal representative.
   - (C) an exact copy.
   - (D) the smallest amount possible.

9. When people **vacate** an apartment, they
   - (A) move out of it.
   - (B) ruin it.
   - (C) change it to make it better.
   - (D) refuse to leave it.

10. A **violation** is
   - (A) an act of violence.
   - (B) the breaking of a rule or law.
   - (C) a musical instrument.
   - (D) an agreement.

11. To **scrutinize** something is to
   - (A) forget it.
   - (B) change its shape.
   - (C) look at it closely.
   - (D) mark over it.

12. **Legislation** is
   - (A) a law or group of laws.
   - (B) part of a cliff.
   - (C) an unbelievable story.
   - (D) clothing worn over the legs.

B Study the Spelling

Word List					
scrutinize	unsightly	minimum	adjacent	vacate	mediate
legislation	compulsory	violation	mutual	oblivious	degrade

Write *legislation*, *oblivious*, *unsightly*, and *compulsory* in alphabetical order. Use dots between the syllables.

1. _____   3. _____

2. _____   4. _____

Write the list word or words for each clue.

5. It is formed from the word *legislate*. _____

6. They end with *ate*. _____   _____

7. The word *grade* is part of its spelling. _____

8. They each have two *a*'s and one *e*.

_____   _____

9. It is formed from the word *violate*. _____

10. There are three *m*'s and one *n* in its spelling. _____

11. The word *cent* is part of its spelling. _____

12. It begins with the *un-* prefix and ends with *-ly*. _____

13. It begins with three consonants. _____

14. It begins like *mutiny* and ends like *usual*. _____

15. The second syllable is *tin*. _____

16. The word *mediation* is formed from this word. _____

One word in each group is misspelled. Circle the misspelled word, and then write it correctly.

17. unsightly   adjecent   mediate   _____

18. compulsury   scrutinize   degrade   _____

19. legislation   mutual   oblivius   _____

20. minimum   vacate   violasion   _____

Score: ◻/20

C Build Your Skills

Language Tutor

The **-ion** suffix changes a word from an action word to a naming word.

Simply add the **-ion** suffix to some action words:

except   except<u>ion</u>

Note the following rules and examples.

Drop the final **e** when adding **-ion** to some action words:

mediate   mediat<u>ion</u>

Notice that the spelling of the action word sometimes changes in other ways:

explore   explor<u>ation</u>

Write these sentences. Add -ion to the underlined action word to form the missing naming word.

1. Do not <u>violate</u> the rules. Any _____ will be punished severely.

_____

2. Congress must <u>legislate</u> new laws. The _____ must be signed by the governor.

_____

3. They plan to <u>invite</u> us over for dinner. Their _____ arrived yesterday.

_____

4. I <u>admire</u> the work she did for the homeless. The more I learn, the more my _____ increases.

_____

5. <u>Combine</u> the oil and vinegar. This _____ will make a tasty salad dressing.

_____

Ⓓ Proofread and Write

Hector wrote this letter to get information on an apartment. He made four spelling mistakes. Cross out the misspelled words. Write the correct spellings above them.

389 Weston Avenue

Muncie, IN 47303

October 17, 1997

Manager

Parkside Apartments

902 Murphy Way

Muncie, IN 47304

Dear Manager:

I must vacate my present apartment in December. I am looking for a new apartment in your part of town. Although I have not scrutanized them, your apartments appear quite lovely. I especially like the ones adjasent to the park. Unlike so many apartments these days, they seem free of unsightly trash containers.

If we can agree on a time of muchual convenience, I would like the chance to see any available apartments. In the meantime I have two questions. What is the minamum rent for a one-bedroom apartment? Is there a compulsory security deposit?

I look forward to hearing from you soon.

Sincerely,

Hector Ruiz

Hector Ruiz

Writing Portfolio

Write a letter to an apartment manager. Use your own paper. Ask for information about the apartments. Use at least four list words.

Proofread your letter carefully and correct any mistakes. Then make a clean copy and send it to the apartment manager or put it in your writing portfolio.

Unit 1 Review

Finish the Meaning

Fill in the circle next to the word that best completes each sentence.

Sample

The plane will be late. The _____ was caused by bad weather.

- ● delay
- (C) worry
- (B) rain
- (D) angry

---

1. When the brothers could not agree, Sid offered to _____ the dispute.

   - (A) vacate
   - (C) mediate
   - (B) thwart
   - (D) forfeit

2. His _____ report was six pages longer than it needed to be.

   - (A) unsightly
   - (C) erratic
   - (B) prudent
   - (D) verbose

3. The instructions were quite _____. We could not misunderstand them.

   - (A) explicit
   - (C) pedestrian
   - (B) fundamental
   - (D) mutual

4. Some assignments are optional, but most are _____.

   - (A) unsightly
   - (C) erratic
   - (B) compulsory
   - (D) prudent

5. The airline tries to _____ new customers with low prices.

   - (A) entice
   - (C) thwart
   - (B) pose
   - (D) degrade

6. Our family never _____ from tradition. We always have turkey on Thanksgiving.

   - (A) assures
   - (C) deviates
   - (B) procures
   - (D) depletes

7. When working on an important project, Kirk is _____ to everything around him.

   - (A) verbose
   - (C) explicit
   - (B) prudent
   - (D) oblivious

8. The uses of the telephone have _____ greatly since its invention.

   - (A) proliferated
   - (C) deviated
   - (B) vacated
   - (D) procured

9. My oven is broken; the temperature _____ between hot and cold.

   - (A) dispenses
   - (C) poses
   - (B) fluctuates
   - (D) entices

10. We will try to _____ tickets to the World Series this year.

    - (A) analyze
    - (C) surrender
    - (B) insist
    - (D) procure

GO ON ➡

Check the Spelling

Fill in the circle next to the word that is spelled correctly and best completes each sentence.

Sample

You must _____ honestly to questions on a tax return.

Ⓐ raspond   Ⓒ respund

● respond   Ⓓ respound

11. This job is too difficult to be done by a _____.

   Ⓐ novise   Ⓒ nawvice

   Ⓑ novice   Ⓓ noviss

12. Many people find the bus the most _____ way to get to work.

   Ⓐ expedient   Ⓒ expiedent

   Ⓑ expeadient   Ⓓ expediunt

13. Before signing a contract, always _____ the fine print.

   Ⓒ screwtinize   Ⓒ scrutinize

   Ⓑ scrutinice   Ⓓ scrutineyes

14. The cart was too large to _____ around the warehouse.

   Ⓐ manoover   Ⓒ maneuvre

   Ⓑ maneveur   Ⓓ maneuver

15. A dentist must have the right _____ to perform his work.

   Ⓐ aparratus   Ⓒ apparatus

   Ⓑ aparattus   Ⓓ apparates

16. Greg usually has breakfast at the coffee shop _____ to the plant.

   Ⓐ ajacent   Ⓒ adjacent

   Ⓑ adjacint   Ⓓ ajaycent

17. The band was so good, we could not _____ from dancing.

   Ⓐ refrane   Ⓒ refrayn

   Ⓑ refrain   Ⓓ refrian

18. Wearing a seatbelt will reduce your risk of becoming a _____ in an accident.

   Ⓐ casualty   Ⓒ casualtie

   Ⓑ causalty   Ⓓ casulty

19. Tina tried to _____ her letter from the mailbox because she had used the wrong address.

   Ⓐ retreive   Ⓒ retrieve

   Ⓑ reteeve   Ⓓ ratrieve

20. You may not always succeed, but you can always _____ to do your best.

   Ⓐ endaevor   Ⓒ endeavur

   Ⓑ endevour   Ⓓ endeavor

STOP

Score: _____ / 20

Healthy Habits

Ⓐ Check the Meaning

Read the paragraphs below. Think about the meaning of the words in bold type.

You probably know that certain actions, such as smoking, have a bad effect on your health. However, other actions can have good effects. For example, **vaccines** can prevent many childhood diseases like measles and polio. Many communities will **inoculate** children free of charge before the school year begins. These simple injections will safeguard them, usually for life. If you have older family members, they may benefit from other types of vaccines. Some diseases, like the flu, are just unpleasant for most people. They can be deadly, though, to a person who is old or **frail**. Vaccines can protect the people you love.

Cleanliness is another habit that can help you and your family stay healthy. Always wash your hands before and after eating or preparing food. You will wash off many germs before they can **contaminate** the food or kitchen areas. Also, wash any cuts or wounds. Wash **superficial** scrapes as well as deep cuts. Use soap and water and an **antiseptic** cream or spray if possible. This keeps germs out of the wound and prevents later **complications**, such as redness, swelling, and other signs of **inflammation**.

Pay attention to your family's mental as well as physical health. Mental illness can cause physical and **emotional** changes. In fact, a mental illness may **masquerade** as a physical disease. A doctor may discover it while looking for something else. Everyone gets sad at times. A person who is **despondent** for months may have a mental illness, such as **depression**. Mental illness can affect anyone, including children and elderly people.

Check the Meaning

Choose the correct meaning for the word in bold type. Fill in the circle next to the correct meaning.

1. An **emotional** change
- Ⓐ is not serious.
- Ⓑ lasts a short time.
- Ⓒ affects the feelings.
- Ⓓ is not noticed.

2. To **inoculate** is to
- Ⓐ invite to a gathering.
- Ⓑ protect against disease.
- Ⓒ examine for a specific purpose.
- Ⓓ report to the authorities.

3. A person who is **despondent** is
- Ⓐ ready to answer questions.
- Ⓑ unclean.
- Ⓒ willing to take risks.
- Ⓓ extremely unhappy.

4. If something is **antiseptic**, it
- Ⓐ is caused by germs.
- Ⓑ makes a cut worse.
- Ⓒ fights germs.
- Ⓓ learns quickly.

5. Depression is
- Ⓐ a mental illness.
- Ⓑ a colorful design.
- Ⓒ extreme poverty.
- Ⓓ a brilliant idea.

6. A **complication** is
- Ⓐ a funny story.
- Ⓑ an added problem.
- Ⓒ a kind of medicine.
- Ⓓ a type of cure.

7. An **inflammation** is
- Ⓐ something that does not burn.
- Ⓑ a medical treatment.
- Ⓒ a type of cut.
- Ⓓ a redness and swelling caused by infection.

8. To **masquerade** is to
- Ⓐ look or act like something else.
- Ⓑ rub repeatedly.
- Ⓒ sleep.
- Ⓓ catch a rare disease.

9. People use **vaccines** to
- Ⓐ cure disease.
- Ⓑ name a disease.
- Ⓒ discover new diseases.
- Ⓓ prevent disease.

10. A **frail** person is
- Ⓐ mentally ill.
- Ⓑ young.
- Ⓒ weak.
- Ⓓ tall.

11. When people **contaminate** something, they
- Ⓐ keep it in one place.
- Ⓑ make it dirty or foul.
- Ⓒ double it.
- Ⓓ raise it up.

12. If something is **superficial**, it is
- Ⓐ shallow or near the surface.
- Ⓑ on top of something else.
- Ⓒ extremely powerful.
- Ⓓ official.

Score: ___ / 12

B Study the Spelling

Word List

| masquerade | emotional | vaccine | inflammation | despondent | antiseptic |
| depression | superficial | frail | complication | contaminate | inoculate |

Write the list word or words for each clue.

1. They end with *tion*. _____ _____

2. It begins like *superior* and ends like *official*. _____

3. They end with *ate*. _____ _____

4. They have a double consonant in their spelling. _____

_____ _____

5. It is formed from the word *emotion*. _____

6. It begins like *masque* and ends like *parade*. _____

7. It has one syllable and rhymes with *snail*. _____

8. It begins like *despair* and ends like *correspondent*. _____

9. It begins with the prefix *anti-*. _____

10. It is formed from the word *depress*. _____

Add the missing syllable. Write the list word.

11. mas_____ade _____

12. _____pondent _____

13. in_____ulate _____

14. contam_____nate _____

15. super_____cial _____

One word in each group is misspelled. Circle the misspelled word, then write it correctly.

16. innoculate   vaccine   despondent   _____

17. complication   depression frayl   _____

18. masquerade   anteseptic contaminate   _____

C Build Your Skills

Language Tutor

A root is a word part that has meaning but may not be able to stand alone as a word. When a prefix is added to the beginning of a root, it changes the meaning of the root.

The *anti-* prefix adds "against" or "opposite" to the meaning of a root. The *super-* prefix adds "above," "over," or "on" to the meaning of a root.

antiwar	against war	antiseptic	against germs
supernatural	above the natural	superficial	on the surface

Write the word in the box next to its meaning. Then write a sentence using the word.

antimagnetic	supervise	supersensitive
superimpose	antisocial	antidepressant

_____ **1.** opposed to or against accepted social practices

_____

_____ **2.** to put on top of something

_____

_____ **3.** to look over the work of someone else

_____

_____ **4.** made to resist a magnetic pull

_____

_____ **5.** a medication used to reduce depression

_____

_____ **6.** extremely sensitive

_____

Score: ◻ / 6

Ⓓ Proofread and Write

The following signs were created for a health fair. The signs have four spelling mistakes. Cross out the misspelled words. Write the correct spellings above them.

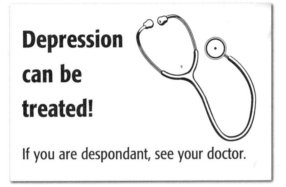

Flu vacine is available now!

See your doctor or

go to the clinic.

The flu can be serious for elderly or frail persons.

Always use an antiseptic
solution to clean cuts.

*Even superfisial cuts can
result in serious inflamation.*

Depression can be treated!

If you are despondant, see your doctor.

Handle all bandages carefully.

Don't let dirt and germs
contaminate them.

Write some ideas for some signs for a health fair. Use at least four list words. Then make the signs on your own paper.

_____

_____

_____

_____

_____

Writing Portfolio

Proofread your signs carefully and correct any mistakes. Then make clean copies and put them in your writing portfolio.

Managing Medical Costs

Ⓐ Check the Meaning

Read the paragraphs below. Think about the meaning of the words in bold type.

A smart shopper can do several things to avoid the high cost of medicines. For a minor **malady**, such as a sore throat, your doctor may write a prescription for an **antibiotic** to attack the infection. The price of this medicine can vary from one **pharmacy** to another. Shop around for the best price. Ask your doctor if you can use a **generic** drug. By avoiding brand-name drugs, you can save money.

If you or someone in your family has a **chronic** disease, such as high blood pressure or diabetes, you may need to buy medicine for a long period of time. You can save as much as 30 percent by buying through a mail-order **distributor**. Another source of help is your union or local public-assistance agency. They will help you compare costs.

Choose the correct meaning for the word in bold type. Fill in the circle next to the correct meaning.

1. A pharmacy is a
- Ⓐ type of music store.
- Ⓑ place that mails packages.
- Ⓒ place to buy prescription medicines.
- Ⓓ person who decides what illness you might have.

2. A generic drug
- Ⓐ does not have a brand name.
- Ⓑ is used to treat high blood pressure.
- Ⓒ does not require a prescription.
- Ⓓ costs more than other drugs.

3. A chronic illness
- Ⓐ lasts for a long time.
- Ⓑ is never serious.
- Ⓒ affects children.
- Ⓓ can be cured with an antibiotic.

4. A malady is
- Ⓐ a loud noise.
- Ⓑ something that affects the memory.
- Ⓒ a disease or disorder of some type.
- Ⓓ a desire to harm someone.

5. A distributor is
- Ⓐ someone who works for the post office.
- Ⓑ a religious figure.
- Ⓒ the money paid for medicine.
- Ⓓ a person or company that sells things.

6. An antibiotic is a
- Ⓐ political party.
- Ⓑ person who helps a doctor.
- Ⓒ medicine used to fight infection.
- Ⓓ place to buy medicine.

Check the Meaning

Insurance can be confusing. Trying to read your policy can leave you confused. Policies may be filled with medical **jargon** and other unfamiliar words. Most policies will include a **concise** summary of what is covered. This part is often easy to understand. If an employer provides the insurance, a phone call to the personnel office may clear things up for you. It is important to **persevere** in your efforts if you wish to take advantage of all your benefits. Some types of health insurance pay for all or part of the costs of prescription drugs. In some cases, the pharmacy **submits** a bill to your insurance company to recover the costs. In others you must complete a form, attach the bill, and send it to your insurance company. The insurance company then **compensates** you for the cost. It is important, therefore, to **retain** the sales receipt and include it with your paperwork.

Choose the correct meaning for the word in bold type. Fill in the circle next to the correct meaning.

7. A **concise** summary is
  Ⓐ written by doctors.
  Ⓑ incomplete.
  Ⓒ short and clear.
  Ⓓ long and confusing.

8. When people **retain** something, they
  Ⓐ forget it.
  Ⓑ have no use for it.
  Ⓒ destroy it.
  Ⓓ keep it.

9. Another word for **compensate** is
  Ⓐ ignore.
  Ⓑ cure.
  Ⓒ pay.
  Ⓓ complain.

10. When people **persevere**, they
  Ⓐ do not give up.
  Ⓑ harm themselves.
  Ⓒ fail.
  Ⓓ injure someone.

11. To **submit** something is to
  Ⓐ hide it.
  Ⓑ hand it in.
  Ⓒ lose it.
  Ⓓ invent it.

12. **Jargon** is
  Ⓐ what you owe someone.
  Ⓑ something that saves you money.
  Ⓒ language used in a certain profession.
  Ⓓ a clear explanation.

B Study the Spelling

Word List

distributor	**jargon**	**antibiotic**	**malady**	**generic**	**concise**
compensate	**retain**	**persevere**	**chronic**	**submit**	**pharmacy**

Write the list word or words for each clue.

1. They end with *ic.* ____________ ____________

____

2. They have two syllables, and each syllable has three letters.

____________ ____________

3. They have two *a*'s in their spelling.

____________ ____________

4. The word *severe* is part of its spelling. ____________

5. It begins with the same sound as *fin*, but it is spelled *ph.*

____

6. It has five syllables. ____________

7. It begins like *compel* and ends like *plate.* ____________

8. It begins with the *re-* prefix. ____________

9. The word *lady* is part of its spelling. ____________

10. It rhymes with *explain.* ____________

Write the list words that come between *change* and *magic* in the dictionary. Write them in alphabetical order.

11. ____________ **14.** ____________

12. ____________ **15.** ____________

13. ____________ **16.** ____________

One word in each group is misspelled. Circle the misspelled word, then write it correctly.

17. antibiotic concice pharmacy ____________

18. generic perseveer compensate ____________

Score: ___ / 18

Language Tutor

Nouns name persons, places, things, or ideas. A proper noun names a particular person, place, thing, or idea. A proper noun always begins with a capital letter. A describing word, or adjective, that is formed from a proper noun also begins with a capital letter and is called a proper adjective.

Common Noun	Proper Noun	Proper Adjective
person	Shakespeare	a Shakespearean actor
country	Mexico	the Mexican government
planet	Mars	Martian invaders

Write these sentences. Capitalize all proper nouns and adjectives.

1. On our trip to california we visited the grand canyon.

_____

2. The chairman called the meeting of the coast guard auxiliary to order.

_____

3. Because the main road was closed, we used tulip avenue.

_____

4. In history class we studied the effects of stalinism.

_____

5. I believe harvard is this nation's oldest university.

_____

6. How has protestantism changed in the past two hundred years?

_____

7. I bought charcoal at valumart hardware.

_____

8. When enrique moved here from puerto rico, he americanized his name.

_____

D Proofread and Write

Jack listened carefully when his employer explained his insurance benefits. He summarized what he heard with these notes from the meeting. Jack made four spelling mistakes. Cross out the misspelled words. Write the correct spellings above them.

> The company's health insurance covers half the cost of all office visits to a doctor. If you have a chronic condition or a serious malady, the company retanes the right to get an opinion from a second doctor. You must submet to a physical twice a year. Your prescription medicines will cost you just $5.00, but you must get your medication from an approved pharmecy or distributor. Whenever available, you must use generic drugs. The insurance will compunsate you for the cost of all emergency treatment at any hospital.

Write a summary of the insurance benefits you have or would like to have. Use at least four list words.

_____

_____

_____

_____

_____

Writing Portfolio

Proofread your summary carefully and correct any mistakes. Then make a clean copy and put it in your writing portfolio.

The Dangers of Drugs

Ⓐ Check the Meaning

Read the paragraphs below. Think about the meaning of the words in bold type.

One of the greatest problems in our society is the misuse of drugs. Even legal drugs, such as alcohol and tobacco, present serious threats to health. Misusing drugs can cause an **addiction** that is very difficult to overcome.

Although some people can drink **moderate** amounts of alcohol safely, others are unable to control the amount they use. They can quickly **exceed** the limits of safe use. Alcohol and similar drugs **impair** judgment and **distort** the senses. Alcohol abuse often leads to serious accidents and the loss of lives. Moreover, alcohol and other drugs can destroy or damage vital body organs, causing serious health problems.

A drug addict needs an **intense** program of therapy to overcome the addiction. Local health agencies can provide a **referral** to agencies or clinics that treat drug abuse. Because such programs are **voluntary**, the individual is free to leave at any time. However, these programs have greater success because they demand a personal commitment by the individual. A successful program usually treats the physical addiction as well as any personal circumstances that **underlie** the problem. Gaining **admittance** to a program is just the first step, however. Curing an addiction often **involves** a lifetime effort. Both **persistence** and courage are needed.

Check the Meaning

Choose the correct meaning for the word in bold type. Fill in the circle next to the correct meaning.

1. When people gain **admittance** to something, they
   - (A) receive it.
   - (B) live inside it.
   - (C) enter it.
   - (D) recommend it highly.

2. Another word for **intense** is
   - (A) extreme.
   - (B) easy.
   - (C) unknown.
   - (D) difficult.

3. A **moderate** amount of something is
   - (A) too small to measure.
   - (B) unusually heavy.
   - (C) twice what is needed.
   - (D) kept within reasonable limits.

4. When people receive a **referral**, they are
   - (A) tried for a crime.
   - (B) sent to another person or group.
   - (C) treated for a problem.
   - (D) given answers to their questions.

5. An **addiction** is a
   - (A) type of math problem.
   - (B) dependence on the regular use of a drug.
   - (C) long, important speech.
   - (D) shortened form of a word.

6. To **distort** is to
   - (A) dream.
   - (B) ask for help.
   - (C) twist out of normal shape.
   - (D) help someone.

7. To **exceed** something is to
   - (A) go beyond its limit.
   - (B) take it to a doctor.
   - (C) break it.
   - (D) put it in front of something else.

8. When people show **persistence**, about something, they
   - (A) stop quickly.
   - (B) stay calm.
   - (C) act cruelly.
   - (D) keep trying.

9. If something is **voluntary**, it is
   - (A) secret.
   - (B) difficult to do.
   - (C) unlikely.
   - (D) a matter of choice.

10. To **underlie** is to
    - (A) tell a lie.
    - (B) be the hidden cause of.
    - (C) draw a line beneath.
    - (D) cure.

11. Another word for **impair** is
    - (A) treat.
    - (B) complete.
    - (C) determine.
    - (D) weaken.

12. To **involve** is to
    - (A) explain.
    - (B) include as a part.
    - (C) look inside.
    - (D) set free.

B Study the Spelling

Word List

impair	underlie	addiction	referral	admittance	involve
distort	moderate	voluntary	exceed	persistence	intense

Write the list word or words for each clue.

1. It begins with the *im-* prefix. _____

2. They have a double consonant in their spelling. _____

_____   _____

3. It has four syllables. _____

4. It is formed from the word *admit*. _____

5. It begins with the *ex-* prefix. _____

6. They begin with the *in-* prefix.

_____   _____

7. It begins like *volume* and ends like *sedentary*. _____

8. Change the first two letters in *revolve* to make this word.

_____

9. It has a double vowel in its spelling. _____

10. It begins like *modern* and ends like *plate*. _____

11. It is formed from the word *refer*. _____

12. It begins like *dissolve* and ends like *extort*. _____

13. It has three syllables and is formed from two smaller words.

_____

Add the missing letters. Write the list word.

14. a___dic___ion _____

15. underl___ ___ _____

16. persist___n___e _____

Score: / 16

C Build Your Skills

Language Tutor

In a one-syllable word, a final consonant that follows a single vowel is doubled before adding an ending that begins with a vowel.

beg + -ed = begged   win + -ing = winning

slip + -ery = slippery   beg + -ar = beggar

In words of two or more syllables, a final consonant that follows a single vowel is doubled before such an ending only if the final syllable in the word is stressed.

suffer + -ing = suffering   admit + -ance = admittance

garden + -er = gardener   refer + -al = referral

Add the ending to each word. Double the final consonant as needed.

1. spoil   +   -ing   =   _____

2. propel   +   -er   =   _____

3. seal   +   -ed   =   _____

4. omit   +   -ed   =   _____

5. begin   +   -ing   =   _____

6. regret   +   -able   =   _____

7. occur   +   -ence   =   _____

8. confer   +   -ed   =   _____

9. prefer   +   -ed   =   _____

10. gossip +   -ing   =   _____

11. forbid +   -en   =   _____

12. develop +   -ed   =   _____

13. repel   +   -ent   =   _____

14. brag   +   -ing   =   _____

15. patrol +   -ed   =   _____

16. deposit +   -ed   =   _____

Ⓓ Proofread and Write

The following posters were made for Drug Awareness Week. The posters have four spelling mistakes.
Cross out the misspelled words. Write the correct spellings above them.

Do not let anyone distort the facts.

Alcohol is a drug and its use
can lead to an adiction.

Do not drink and drive.
Even a moderite
use of alcohol can impair
your abilities.

Never excede the
recommended
use of a medicine.

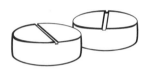

When fighting a drug problem,

persistance pays off!

Write some advice to someone about using drugs. It can be in the form of a poster or a letter. Use at
least four list words.

_____

_____

_____

_____

_____

_____

_____

Writing Portfolio

Proofread your advice and correct any mistakes. Make a full-size poster or a
clean copy of the letter and mail it. If you prefer, make a clean copy and put it in
your writing portfolio.

Seeing the Doctor

A Check the Meaning

Read the paragraph below. Think about the meaning of the words in bold type.

Getting treatment for an illness or injury often begins with filling out a form. These forms ask for a wide **variety** of information. They usually ask about your medical history, insurance coverage, and the expected method of payment. There may also be some **miscellaneous** questions about your family and job. If you anticipate such questions, you can prepare for them and **accelerate** the process. For example, most medical offices ask for your Social Security Number and the group or plan number of your insurance. If you do not have insurance, you may need to provide a credit card number and the date it **expires**. You will also be asked to list any serious illnesses you have had and any medicines you are now taking. This information is **indispensable** since it affects how doctors **diagnose** and treat your problem. Keeping this information handy will get you better and faster treatment.

Choose the correct meaning for the word in bold type. Fill in the circle next to the correct meaning.

1. Another word for **miscellaneous** is
- Ⓐ mixed.
- Ⓑ confused.
- Ⓒ unreasonable.
- Ⓓ sick.

2. To **expire** means to
- Ⓐ sign up.
- Ⓑ attack.
- Ⓒ come to an end.
- Ⓓ require payment.

3. A **variety** is a
- Ⓐ soft cloth.
- Ⓑ group of many different things.
- Ⓒ necessary item.
- Ⓓ hard surface.

4. If something is **indispensable**, it is
- Ⓐ silent.
- Ⓑ not costly.
- Ⓒ hard to find.
- Ⓓ absolutely necessary.

5. To **accelerate** something is to
- Ⓐ speed it up.
- Ⓑ repair it.
- Ⓒ begin to work on it.
- Ⓓ make it happy.

6. To **diagnose** is to
- Ⓐ charge for treatment.
- Ⓑ send away.
- Ⓒ follow directions.
- Ⓓ identify an illness.

Check the Meaning

Read the paragraph below. Think about the meaning of the words in bold type.

No one really likes going to the doctor, even though it is the **sensible** thing to do when feeling ill. Most people tend to **postpone** making an appointment in the hope that things will get better in a day or two. Yet a common cold or mild case of the flu can sometimes be discussed with a doctor over the telephone. Bed rest and a lot of liquids may be the best treatment. However, the sooner a person reports any **abnormal** conditions to a doctor, the sooner he or she can **intervene** and treat the problem. Any illness that lasts longer than a day or includes a fever should be looked at. Early treatment may **impede** the progress of an illness and **curtail** its spread to other family members. It is always best to contact a doctor. Doctors should decide whether their patients need appointments.

Choose the correct meaning for the word in bold type. Fill in the circle next to the correct meaning.

7. When people **postpone** something, they
- Ⓐ announce it publicly.
- Ⓑ put it off until later.
- Ⓒ mail it.
- Ⓓ remember to do it.

8. To **intervene** is to
- Ⓐ introduce.
- Ⓑ balance carefully.
- Ⓒ ask questions.
- Ⓓ come between or change.

9. When people **curtail** something, they
- Ⓐ spread it quickly.
- Ⓑ give it away.
- Ⓒ cut it short or reduce it.
- Ⓓ move it about.

10. Another word for **sensible** is
- Ⓐ reasonable.
- Ⓑ exciting.
- Ⓒ healthy.
- Ⓓ heavy.

11. An **abnormal** condition is one that is
- Ⓐ common.
- Ⓑ not normal.
- Ⓒ illegal.
- Ⓓ expensive to treat.

12. When people **impede** the progress of something, they
- Ⓐ blow it up.
- Ⓑ improve it.
- Ⓒ slow it down.
- Ⓓ recommend it to others.

Score: / 12

B Study the Spelling

Word List

variety	indispensable	expire	postpone	diagnose	abnormal
curtail	miscellaneous	impede	intervene	sensible	accelerate

Write the list words with two syllables. Use a dot between the syllables.

1. _____   3. _____

2. _____   4. _____

Write the list words with three syllables. Use dots between the syllables.

5. _____   7. _____

6. _____   8. _____

Write the list word or words for each clue.

9. It has five syllables and a double consonant. _____

10. They end with *ble*. _____   _____

11. It has four syllables and a double consonant. _____

12. Its abbreviation is *misc*. _____

13. It has two syllables. Both syllables begin with the same letter.

_____

14. There is an *ie* in its spelling. _____

15. It begins like *impeach* and ends like *recede*. _____

16. The word *nose* is part of its spelling. _____

Add the missing syllable. Write a list word.

17. ac_____erate   _____

18. _____tail   _____

19. indispen_____ble   _____

20. inter_____   _____

Ⓒ Build Your Skills

Language Tutor

A root is a word part that has meaning but may not be able to stand alone as a word. When a prefix is added to the beginning of a root, it changes or adds to the meaning of the root.

The *ex-* prefix adds "out of" or "from" to the meaning of a root.

The prefixes *im-* and *in-* add "not" to the meaning of a root.

ex- + pire = expire	to run out of time; to end
in- + dispensable = indispensable	not able to do without; necessary
im- + pede = impede	to slow or delay; not allowing easy movement

Write the word from the box next to its meaning.

expel	imperfect	exclude	exhaust	impersonal
extinct	impatient	impolite	immune	insubordinate

_____ **1.** not for any one person; not personal

_____ **2.** having faults and defects; not perfect

_____ **3.** to keep out

_____ **4.** not accepting of authority

_____ **5.** not considerate

_____ **6.** to wear out

_____ **7.** to drive or force out

_____ **8.** not able to wait

_____ **9.** not able to be infected

_____ **10.** not living any longer

Score: ⟋ 10

Ⓓ Proofread and Write

Ramon needed to enter a hospital for some tests. He was asked to give his medical history on a form. This is what Ramon wrote. He made four spelling mistakes. Cross out the misspelled words. Write the correct spellings above them.

> I eat three sensable meals a day, but I still gain an abnormal amount of weight. In June I had to curtale my daily exercises. This will impede my plan for losing my extra weight. I have always felt that exercise is an indispensable part of good health.
>
> I have never had a doctor diagnoze a serious problem, but I have had a variety of miscellanous minor illnesses. Once I had to postpone a vacation because of the flu.

Write your own medical history or the medical history of an imaginary person. Use at least four list words.

_____

_____

_____

_____

_____

_____

Writing Portfolio

Proofread your medical history and correct any mistakes. Then make a clean copy and put it in your writing portfolio.

Unit 2 Review

Finish the Meaning

Fill in the circle next to the word that best completes each sentence.

1. I need to renew my driver's license before it _____ next month.

   Ⓐ rotates   Ⓒ expires
   Ⓑ distorts   Ⓓ deviates

2. Weeks of rainy weather can make even the most cheerful people _____.

   Ⓐ sensible   Ⓒ oblivious
   Ⓑ despondent   Ⓓ moderate

3. The best business memos are _____ and to the point.

   Ⓐ intense   Ⓒ emotional
   Ⓑ verbose   Ⓓ concise

4. Poor equipment can _____ your ability to do a good job.

   Ⓐ impair   Ⓒ postpone
   Ⓑ retain   Ⓓ procure

5. When lawyers get together, they sometimes use _____ only they can understand.

   Ⓐ legislation   Ⓒ transactions
   Ⓑ jargon   Ⓓ apparatuses

6. A broken mirror can _____ your appearance.

   Ⓐ diagnose   Ⓒ distort
   Ⓑ dispense   Ⓓ entice

7. I love the great _____ of fruits and vegetables available in the summer.

   Ⓐ endeavor   Ⓒ masquerade
   Ⓑ addiction   Ⓓ variety

8. A broken fuel line might _____ the lake.

   Ⓐ curtail   Ⓒ surrender
   Ⓑ contaminate   Ⓓ retrieve

9. Many people suffer their entire lives from _____ back pain.

   Ⓐ moderate   Ⓒ generic
   Ⓑ chronic   Ⓓ mutual

10. The company hopes workers will choose to participate in the _____ exercise program.

    Ⓐ voluntary   Ⓒ compulsory
    Ⓑ antibiotic   Ⓓ prudent

11. The government will _____ if the strike is not settled soon.

    Ⓐ proliferate   Ⓒ insist
    Ⓑ intervene   Ⓓ refrain

12. A _____ wound usually heals faster than a deep cut.

    Ⓐ sensible   Ⓒ frail
    Ⓑ superficial   Ⓓ verbose

GO ON

Check the Spelling

Choose the word that is spelled correctly and best completes each sentence.

13. A good road map is _____ when traveling in an unfamiliar area.

    (A) indespensable   (C) indispensable

    (B) indespensible   (D) indispensible

14. The company nurse will _____ anyone who has not yet had a flu shot.

    (A) innoculate   (C) inoculate

    (B) inocculate   (D) inoculait

15. Monitor your budget so that you do not _____ your spending limits.

    (A) exceed   (C) exede

    (B) excead   (D) exeede

16. The most successful people are those who _____ until they meet their goals.

    (A) presevere   (C) persevier

    (B) pursevere   (D) persevere

17. Clean all food preparation areas with an _____ cleaner.

    (A) anteseptic   (C) antiseptik

    (B) antiseptic   (D) antiseptick

18. Insurance may reduce your medical costs, but it will not _____ you for travel expenses.

    (A) compensate   (C) compensait

    (B) compinsate   (D) cumpensate

19. When you need a specialist, it is good to get a _____ from someone you trust.

    (A) referral   (C) referrul

    (B) refferal   (D) refirral

20. A lack of exercise will _____ the aging process.

    (A) acellerate   (C) accelarate

    (B) acelerrate   (D) accelerate

21. Many people have a junk drawer for rubber bands, pencils, and _____ things.

    (A) miscellanious   (C) missellaneous

    (B) miscellaneous   (D) micscellaneous

22. Keep trying; _____ almost always pays off.

    (A) persitence   (C) persistence

    (B) persistance   (D) pursistence

23. A head cold is a common winter _____.

    (A) malidy   (C) mallady

    (B) maladie   (D) malady

24. An _____ near a cut may be a sign of infection.

    (A) inflamation   (C) infleation

    (B) innflamation   (D) inflammation

STOP

Working Together

Ⓐ Check the Meaning

Read the paragraphs below. Think about the meaning of the words in bold type.

A century ago, most people worked on farms or in small shops. Little teamwork was demanded of workers. In today's offices, department stores, and factories, things are different. Teamwork is **imperative**. Working well with others is a vital job skill.

There are several keys to successful teamwork. Respect, good manners, and thoughtful behavior are fundamental to creating a **humane**, pleasant environment. To maintain such an environment, employers cannot **abide** certain kinds of behavior. Arriving late or refusing to accept responsibility for getting the job done are behaviors that will soon **undermine** morale. Workers cannot accomplish much when there is **dissension** among them.

A supervisor may overlook an occasional **breach** of good manners. Under stress, a worker might understandably make an **impertinent** remark. However, a worker who continues to **harass** others would cause more serious trouble. Such a **habitual** troublemaker can threaten an entire project. Worse still, such a worker can **discredit** an entire company.

Teamwork is one quality supervisors always consider when they **assess** a worker's performance. They look for employees who support each other, take pride in their work, and **foster** a positive working atmosphere.

Check the Meaning

Choose the correct meaning for the word in bold type. Fill in the circle next to the correct meaning.

1. An **impertinent** remark is one that is
   - Ⓐ important.
   - Ⓑ independent.
   - Ⓒ rude or insulting.
   - Ⓓ lazy.

2. If something is **imperative**, it is
   - Ⓐ quiet.
   - Ⓑ unable to be repaired.
   - Ⓒ hidden from view.
   - Ⓓ urgent and necessary.

3. Another word for **dissension** is
   - Ⓐ disagreement.
   - Ⓑ friendship.
   - Ⓒ enjoyment.
   - Ⓓ disease.

4. If you **abide** something, you
   - Ⓐ eat it.
   - Ⓑ enjoy it.
   - Ⓒ allow it.
   - Ⓓ get better at it.

5. If you **harass** workers, you
   - Ⓐ help them succeed.
   - Ⓑ bother them.
   - Ⓒ listen to them.
   - Ⓓ compare them to others.

6. To be **humane** is to be
   - Ⓐ under stress.
   - Ⓑ lonely.
   - Ⓒ kind.
   - Ⓓ boring.

7. A **breach** is
   - Ⓐ an explanation.
   - Ⓑ a funny remark.
   - Ⓒ a reward.
   - Ⓓ a break or violation.

8. Another word for **undermine** is
   - Ⓐ dig.
   - Ⓑ weaken.
   - Ⓒ succeed.
   - Ⓓ steal.

9. If you **discredit** something, you
   - Ⓐ take it back.
   - Ⓑ loan it money.
   - Ⓒ divide it into parts.
   - Ⓓ disgrace it.

10. To **assess** something is to
    - Ⓐ sell it.
    - Ⓑ make a judgment about it.
    - Ⓒ testify about it.
    - Ⓓ write a report about it.

11. Another word for **habitual** is
    - Ⓐ angry.
    - Ⓑ dangerous.
    - Ⓒ regular.
    - Ⓓ old.

12. If you **foster** something, you
    - Ⓐ send it away.
    - Ⓑ encourage it.
    - Ⓒ challenge it.
    - Ⓓ improve it.

Score: /12

B Study the Spelling

Word List

abide	foster	impertinent	imperative	discredit	humane
assess	harass	undermine	dissension	habitual	breach

Write the list word or words for each clue.

1. They end with a double consonant.

   _____ _____

2. Add a letter to *human* to make this word. _____

3. They begin with the *im-* prefix.

   _____ _____

4. Add a prefix to *credit* to make this word. _____

5. It is formed from the word *habit*. _____

6. It has one syllable. It begins and ends with two consonants.

   _____

7. It has three syllables and three *s*'s. _____

8. It is made from two words, and it begins and ends with a vowel.

   _____

9. It has two syllables. The first syllable is one letter. _____

10. Change one letter in *faster* to make this word. _____

Circle the list word in each of these words. Then write the list word.

11. harassment _____

12. assessment _____

13. discredited _____

Add the missing syllable. Write the list word.

14. un_____mine _____

15. impera_____ _____

16. har_____ _____

© Build Your Skills

Language Tutor

The *dis-* prefix can add several different meanings to a root. It usually adds a negative meaning, such as "no," "not," or "not any."

discredit   to cause the loss of someone's reputation

dissension   lack of agreement

dissimilar   not alike; different

Add a word with the *dis-* prefix from the box to complete each sentence. Write the sentence.

disloyal	**discount**	**disrupt**
distract	**disrepair**	**disclose**

1. My club gets a 15 percent _____ on every item.

_____

2. The magician would never _____ the secret of his trick.

_____

3. The soldier was accused of being _____ to his country.

_____

4. A protester tried to _____ the meeting.

_____

5. The old house was in a state of _____.

_____

6. Do not let the noise _____ you during the test.

_____

Ⓓ Proofread and Write

Lia was asked to talk to her fellow workers about the importance of teamwork. She made the following notes to use in her talk. She made four spelling mistakes. Cross out the misspelled words. Write the correct spellings above them.

To work well with others, you must abide by certain simple rules:

1. Asess problems as a group and try to agree on a solution. This will fostar goodwill.

2. If you make a mistake, it is imperative that you admit to it. Trying to deny it will only discredit you.

3. One impertinant remark will undermine the trust of your partners and create disension.

4. We spend a big part of our life on the job. Work to create a humane environment.

Write a list of your own rules for getting along with others at work. Use at least four list words.

_____

_____

_____

_____

_____

Writing Portfolio

Proofread your list carefully and correct any mistakes. Then make a clean copy and put it in your writing portfolio.

Sharing Information

Ⓐ Check the Meaning

Read the paragraph below. Think about the meaning of the words in bold type.

Most of the day is spent listening or speaking. Clear and accurate **verbal** communication is particularly important in the workplace. When someone attempts to **convey** information over the telephone, keep your mind on the message. Do not try to talk with someone in the room as well. Before you hang up, **ascertain** all the information you need. For example, suppose you are asked to deliver a package to someone in another building. You need to know exactly how to get there and when to deliver it. Make notes to help you remember the key information. Then **confirm** the information by reading it back to the caller. If the caller is uncertain, take the **initiative** and find out what you need to know. Ask clear, precise questions that will get a **definitive** answer. Most important, ask people who might know the answer. A security guard will know the location of a building. A mail room worker will know where to find a particular person.

Choose the correct meaning for the word in bold type. Fill in the circle next to the correct meaning.

1. If you **ascertain** something, you
   - Ⓐ hang it up.
   - Ⓑ hide it from others.
   - Ⓒ receive it.
   - Ⓓ find out about it.

2. To **convey** is to
   - Ⓐ offer or sell.
   - Ⓑ carry or communicate.
   - Ⓒ direct.
   - Ⓓ clarify.

3. If you take the **initiative**, you
   - Ⓐ take the leading role.
   - Ⓑ ruin a project.
   - Ⓒ follow another person.
   - Ⓓ accept an invitation.

4. A **definitive** answer is
   - Ⓐ given in a loud voice.
   - Ⓑ complete and final.
   - Ⓒ written on paper.
   - Ⓓ not heard.

5. **Verbal** communication uses
   - Ⓐ words.
   - Ⓑ mistakes.
   - Ⓒ a lot of time.
   - Ⓓ machines.

6. To **confirm** is to
   - Ⓐ bless.
   - Ⓑ destroy.
   - Ⓒ make certain.
   - Ⓓ give.

Check the Meaning

Read the paragraph below. Think about the meaning of the words in bold type.

The memos you write at work are different from the letters you send to friends. Because of your **intimate** relationship with a close friend, your writing need not be formal and well organized. You can write about whatever pops into your mind. Such a loosely organized approach will **detract** from a written message at work. Instead, limit the message to one specific purpose and maintain an **objective** point of view. Focus on the job, the problem, or the information you want. Avoid making **derogatory** remarks or expressing your personal feelings. If **feasible,** number the separate steps or the key parts of your message. If you need an answer to a question, provide a response card or page and tell exactly when it should be returned. A timely response to your message will **attest** to the importance of this extra effort.

Choose the correct meaning for the word in bold type. Fill in the circle next to the correct meaning.

7. If something is **feasible,** it is
- Ⓐ possible.
- Ⓑ unbelievable.
- Ⓒ foolish.
- Ⓓ expensive.

8. To **detract** means to
- Ⓐ decide.
- Ⓑ reduce in value.
- Ⓒ stay on course.
- Ⓓ stop doing something.

9. To **attest** is to
- Ⓐ check.
- Ⓑ prove.
- Ⓒ discover.
- Ⓓ refuse.

10. If something is **derogatory,** it
- Ⓐ asks a question.
- Ⓑ is unkind or insulting.
- Ⓒ shows respect.
- Ⓓ shows much thought.

11. Another word for **intimate** is
- Ⓐ occasional.
- Ⓑ silly.
- Ⓒ painful.
- Ⓓ familiar.

12. If you are **objective,** you
- Ⓐ are not influenced by personal feelings.
- Ⓑ often fight with others.
- Ⓒ complain frequently.
- Ⓓ write many letters.

Score: ___ / 12

B Study the Spelling

Word List

verbal	intimate	ascertain	feasible	convey	objective
attest	initiative	derogatory	confirm	detract	definitive

Write the list word for each clue.

1. It has three syllables and ends with *tive*. _____

2. It rhymes with *obey*. _____

3. The word *certain* is part of its spelling. _____

4. There is a double consonant in its spelling. _____

5. The word *verb* is part of its spelling. _____

6. It has six vowels. Four of them are *i*'s. _____

7. Change the prefix in *distract* to make this word. _____

8. The word *firm* is part of its spelling. _____

9. It begins like *feast* and ends like *sensible*. _____

10. It has five syllables. The last syllable is *ry*. _____

Write the list word that comes between each pair of words in alphabetical order.

11. innate _____ introduce

12. copy _____ delay

13. devoid _____ feast

14. pleasant _____ zebra

15. never _____ please

16. detail _____ eager

One word in each group is misspelled. Circle the misspelled word and then write it correctly.

17. objective   atest   confirm   _____

18. derogetory   verbal   detract   _____

19. ascertian   feasible   definitive   _____

20. convay   intimate   initiative   _____

Score: _____ / 20

C Build Your Skills

Language Tutor

A suffix is a word part added to the end of a word. A suffix can change the way the word is used. Adding a suffix to a word or a root can create an adjective, or describing word. Notice the underlined suffixes in the adjectives below.

a feas<u>ible</u> idea   the prob<u>able</u> cause   a studi<u>ous</u> child

an habit<u>ual</u> criminal   a tradition<u>al</u> event   a technic<u>al</u> problem

Add the adjective from the box that best completes each sentence. Then write the sentence.

traceable	**prosperous**	**believable**
valuable	**residential**	**seasonal**

1. Factories cannot be built in _____ areas.

_____

2. The fire's cause was _____ to bad electrical wires.

_____

3. Many people say that her story is not true, but I think it is

_____.

_____

4. We keep our _____ documents in a safe.

_____

5. A _____ merchant made a large contribution.

_____

6. Some fruits are _____, so they are easy to find at certain times of the year.

_____

Score: / 6

Ⓓ Proofread and Write

Pete got the following memo at work. It contains four spelling mistakes. Cross out the misspelled words. Write the correct spellings above them.

MEMO

TO: Pete Travis   **DATE:** 10/29/98

FROM: Maria Sotos

SUBJECT: Parking Problem

Please take the initiative on the parking problem we are having. Try to ascertane whether it is feasable to get more cars in the employee lot. Get a definative count of the number of current users. Confirm your findings with Barbara Cohen, who sells parking permits. She will attest to the number sold this year. Convay your findings to me by Tuesday. I know I can count on a clear, objective report from you on this problem.

Write a memo to someone you work with or might work with in the future. Use at least four list words.

_____

_____

_____

_____

_____

 Writing Portfolio

Proofread your memo and correct any mistakes. Then make a clean copy and put it in your writing portfolio.

11 Important Reading

A Check the Meaning

Read the paragraphs below. Think about the meaning of the words in bold type.

Newly hired employees receive many things to read. They may read flashy leaflets or pages of **dense** print. Because there is so much required reading, some employees are tempted to **dismiss** this material as unimportant. This would be a mistake, however. These documents are **reliable** sources of information about the employer, type of business, and benefits workers may receive. One item employees usually receive is an employee handbook. This book is so important that some companies have employees sign a paper as proof that they received the information. Among other things, this **invaluable** book explains how to seek **redress** for a situation in which a worker feels wronged. It lists several reasons why a company may **terminate** an employee. These often include the use of drugs or alcohol on the job, the theft of company property, and any **deliberate** attempt to hurt the business. For example, an employee who **agitates** fellow workers with constant complaints and arguments may be risking his or her job.

Often the new employee is given a job description and a list of standards for judging job performance. This list may include the **characteristics** of a **proficient** level of performance. This information is important because future pay raises are based on a worker's job performance.

Many new employees are hired on **probation** for an **arbitrary** amount of time, usually from six months to a year. During this time, employees must prove themselves. An employer has the right to terminate an employee who is on probation. New workers will know about probation, benefits, and other information if they read their employee handbooks.

Check the Meaning

Choose the correct meaning for the word in bold type. Fill in the circle next to the correct meaning.

1. If something is **arbitrary**, it
   - Ⓐ is fought over.
   - Ⓑ cannot be explained.
   - Ⓒ is not worth reading.
   - Ⓓ is based on no particular reason.

2. Another word for **reliable** is
   - Ⓐ simple.
   - Ⓑ complicated.
   - Ⓒ dependable.
   - Ⓓ worthless.

3. To **agitate** is to
   - Ⓐ clean thoroughly.
   - Ⓑ change for the better.
   - Ⓒ stir up in a violent manner.
   - Ⓓ create interest.

4. A **deliberate** attempt is
   - Ⓐ done on purpose.
   - Ⓑ quick.
   - Ⓒ unsuccessful.
   - Ⓓ unlawful.

5. If you **dismiss** something, you
   - Ⓐ greet it warmly.
   - Ⓑ put it out of your mind.
   - Ⓒ make a file for it.
   - Ⓓ treat it as very important.

6. People who are **proficient** at a job
   - Ⓐ are proud of it.
   - Ⓑ do it very well.
   - Ⓒ get paid for it.
   - Ⓓ dislike it.

7. Another word for **invaluable** is
   - Ⓐ necessary.
   - Ⓑ certain.
   - Ⓒ predictable.
   - Ⓓ priceless.

8. **Probation** is
   - Ⓐ a test or trial period.
   - Ⓑ an official notice.
   - Ⓒ a group of people.
   - Ⓓ a tool needed to do a job.

9. If something is **dense**, it is
   - Ⓐ written in another language.
   - Ⓑ crowded closely together.
   - Ⓒ easy to read.
   - Ⓓ important to your job.

10. A **characteristic** is
    - Ⓐ an actor in a play.
    - Ⓑ a feature that sets something apart.
    - Ⓒ the virtue of always telling the truth.
    - Ⓓ an unimportant detail.

11. To **terminate** is to
    - Ⓐ agree.
    - Ⓑ enlarge.
    - Ⓒ sell.
    - Ⓓ end.

12. If you seek **redress**, you want
    - Ⓐ a raise in pay.
    - Ⓑ better clothing.
    - Ⓒ more help with a job.
    - Ⓓ something wrong made right.

B Study the Spelling

Word List

agitate	deliberate	reliable	probation	dismiss	characteristic
dense	terminate	redress	proficient	arbitrary	invaluable

Write the list word or words for each clue.

1. They end with a double consonant.

   _____ _____

2. It has one syllable and rhymes with *sense*. _____

3. They end with *ate*. _____ _____

   _____

4. They begin with *re*. _____ _____

5. They begin with the *pro-* prefix.

   _____ _____

6. It is formed from the word *rely*. _____

7. It has four syllables. The last syllable is *y*. _____

8. They end with *able*. _____ _____

9. It comes first in alphabetical order. _____

10. It does not follow the rule "*i* before *e* except after *c*." _____

11. They contain five vowels. _____

   _____ _____

Write the list word from which each word was made.

12. agitation _____

13. probationary _____

14. reliability _____

15. dismissal _____

16. arbitrarily _____

C Build Your Skills

Language Tutor

Most one- and two-syllable words add -er to an adjective when comparing two things and -est when comparing three or more things.

> The boat moved slowly through the *dense* fog.
> The fog was *denser* than it had been the day before.
> It was the *densest* fog the captain had ever seen.

Words of three or more syllables use *more* and *most* when making comparisons. A two-syllable word that is difficult to pronounce when -er or -est is added also uses *more* and *most* when making comparisons.

> The company wants *reliable* workers.
> Joanne is *more reliable* than Dick.
> Oman is the *most reliable* worker in the department.

Remember to drop a final *e*, double a final consonant, or change a final *y* to *i* when necessary.

Write the following sentences. Replace the word in parentheses with the correct word or words to complete the comparison. The first one has been done for you.

1. Mike is (strong) than his brother.

    Mike is stronger than his brother.

2. Our classroom is (noisy) than the library.

_____

3. The computer is the (expensive) thing in the office.

_____

4. Jenny was (ambitious) than Eve, so she worked harder.

_____

5. You could not find a (merry) group of people.

_____

6. The museum has the (early) known example of Navajo pottery.

_____

Score: ◻ / 6

Ⓓ Proofread and Write

Sam wrote this friendly letter to his brother to tell him about his new job. Sam made four spelling mistakes. Cross out the misspelled words. Write the correct spellings above them.

March 20, 1997

Dear Ben,

I just started work at Barb's Trucking Company. Your advice about the interview was an invalueable help. It got me the job. I will be on probation for six months. In that time I must prove to be a relieable driver. Moving a two-ton truck through dense city streets won't be easy. The former driver will train me until I become profishent.

The boss has the characteristics I like in a person. She does not dismiss problems until they are solved and makes an honest attempt to redres any wrong. I hope to work here a long time.

Your grateful brother,

Sam

Write a friendly letter to someone about your job or the job you want to get. Use your own paper. Use at least four list words.

Writing Portfolio

Proofread your letter and correct any mistakes. Then make a clean copy to mail or put in your writing portfolio.

Safety in the Workplace

Ⓐ Check the Meaning

Read the paragraphs below. Think about the meaning of the words in bold type.

Every worker must **strive** to make the workplace safe. Safety begins by observing all rules, especially those for smoking. Workers should be **meticulous** about keeping their areas clean and free of trash. Garbage, especially paper, is a serious fire **hazard**.

Working with dangerous substances carries certain **inherent** risks. Special glasses, shoes, and other protective clothing are usually required. Such clothing may be uncomfortable and awkward to wear. Nevertheless, supervisors must be **adamant** in enforcing the rules on protective clothing.

Supervisors must be **vigilant** when it comes to safety. They must continually educate workers. They should also put up posters in all work areas to remind workers of the rules and procedures.

Choose the correct meaning for the word in bold type. Fill in the circle next to the correct meaning.

1. Another word for **hazard** is
Ⓐ exercise.
Ⓑ choice.
Ⓒ danger.
Ⓓ machine.

2. Another word for **vigilant** is
Ⓐ watchful.
Ⓑ fearful.
Ⓒ angry.
Ⓓ broken.

3. Another word for **adamant** is
Ⓐ silly.
Ⓑ lazy.
Ⓒ firm.
Ⓓ peculiar.

4. If you are **meticulous**, you are
Ⓐ extremely careful.
Ⓑ very intelligent.
Ⓒ cheerful.
Ⓓ honest.

5. An **inherent** risk
Ⓐ comes from one's parents.
Ⓑ is difficult to imagine.
Ⓒ is connected to a specific thing or situation.
Ⓓ is nothing to worry about.

6. To **strive** is to
Ⓐ understand.
Ⓑ solve problems.
Ⓒ read carefully.
Ⓓ try hard.

Check the Meaning

Safety problems arise from many sources. A machine that **malfunctions** can be the source of danger. An overheated machine can start a fire. A loose part can injure the operator. Report any mechanical problems promptly. Most machinery has safeguards for the operator. For example, power saws have covers on the blades. Never **alter** machinery in any way. Trading speed for safety is a bad bargain.

Workers who have been on the job for many years may become **lax** about following safety rules. If they have had no problems in the past, minor **infractions** may seem harmless. A friendly reminder from a fellow worker or supervisor may be all that is needed to **reinforce** the importance of safety. However, a **flagrant** violation of the rules may call for immediate action. Study your company's policy on reporting such problems. It is in everyone's best interest to understand these policies.

Choose the correct meaning for the word in bold type. Fill in the circle next to the correct meaning.

7. Another word for **lax** is
- Ⓐ careful.
- Ⓑ careless.
- Ⓒ hopeful.
- Ⓓ hopeless.

8. A **flagrant** violation is
- Ⓐ small.
- Ⓑ popular.
- Ⓒ clearly outrageous.
- Ⓓ committed secretly.

9. When people **reinforce** something, they
- Ⓐ reduce it.
- Ⓑ divide it.
- Ⓒ ridicule it.
- Ⓓ strengthen it.

10. An **infraction** is
- Ⓐ a mathematical term.
- Ⓑ the breaking of a law or rule.
- Ⓒ an outline.
- Ⓓ a type of safety equipment.

11. If something **malfunctions**, it
- Ⓐ loses its importance.
- Ⓑ is difficult to understand.
- Ⓒ produces dangerous chemicals.
- Ⓓ fails to work properly.

12. Another word for **alter** is
- Ⓐ try.
- Ⓑ receive.
- Ⓒ change.
- Ⓓ avoid.

Score: / 12

B Study the Spelling

Write the list word or words for each clue.

1. It begins with three consonants. _____

2. It begins with the *re-* prefix. _____

3. They have one syllable. _____ _____

4. They have two syllables. The vowel in both syllables is *a*.

_____ _____

5. They have three syllables. The first syllable is *in*.

_____ _____

6. It rhymes with *ridiculous*. _____

7. Change one letter in *tax* to make this word. _____

8. It begins like *also* and ends like *sister*. _____

9. They end with the *–ion* suffix.

_____ _____

10. There are three *a*'s in its spelling. _____

Form a list word by matching the beginning of a word in the first column with the middle and ending in the second and third columns. Write the list word.

in	in	ent	**11.** _____
vig	frac	mant	**12.** _____
ad	i	force	**13.** _____
in	func	lant	**14.** _____
re	her	tion	**15.** _____
mal	a	tion	**16.** _____

Score: ⬜ / 16

© Build Your Skills

Language Tutor

The *mal-* prefix adds "bad" to the meaning of a root.

The *bene-* or *ben-* prefix adds "good" to the meaning of a word or root.

malfunction	to function badly	The copy machine seems to malfunction every time I need something quickly.
benefit	something good; a help	The driver had the benefit of knowing a shortcut.

Read each sentence. Think about the meaning of the underlined word. Then write a short definition of the word.

1. The wealthy <u>benefactor</u> gave a million dollars to the college.

_____

2. Dr. Rice cannot seem to find the cause of her <u>malady</u>.

_____

3. The tests showed that the tumor was <u>malignant</u>.

_____

4. His <u>benign</u> smile could light up an entire room.

_____

5. The candidate claims the story is a <u>malicious</u> lie.

_____

6. After several days without food, the child suffered from <u>malnutrition</u>.

_____

7. No doctor in our town has ever been accused of <u>malpractice</u>.

_____

8. My aunt's will made me the <u>beneficiary</u> of her estate.

_____

Score: ___ / 8

Ⓓ Proofread and Write

The following signs were posted in a lumberyard. The signs contain four spelling mistakes. Cross out the misspelled words. Write the correct spellings above them.

Severe fire hazard.

Smoking prohibited!

Report
any
mechanical
malfuncton
to the
foreman.

Never attempt to
altur or bypass the
safety devices.

Management is adament
about these rules.
A good worker
is a vigilant worker!

Electric current has inherent risks.

Turn off machinery not in use.

Any fragrent violation of this rule is

grounds for dismissal.

Write some safety rules for the place where you work or would like to work. Use at least four list words.

_____

_____

_____

_____

_____

 Writing Portfolio

Proofread your rules and correct any mistakes. Then make a clean copy and put it in your writing portfolio.

Unit 3 Review

Finish the Meaning

Fill in the circle next to the word that best completes each sentence.

1. The report is perfect; I would not _____ a thing.

   Ⓐ retain   Ⓒ alter
   Ⓑ impair   Ⓓ confirm

2. It is _____ that you file a tax return every year.

   Ⓐ imperative   Ⓒ intense
   Ⓑ intimate   Ⓓ abnormal

3. If you do not pay the electric bill, the company may _____ your service.

   Ⓐ reinforce   Ⓒ thwart
   Ⓑ confirm   Ⓓ terminate

4. They have found no _____ cause for the crash.

   Ⓐ definitive   Ⓒ invaluable
   Ⓑ derogatory   Ⓓ impertinent

5. The juror must take an _____ look at all evidence.

   Ⓐ objective   Ⓒ abnormal
   Ⓑ arbitrary   Ⓓ emotional

6. After years of study and practice, Elizabeth has become a _____ violinist.

   Ⓐ deliberate   Ⓒ proficient
   Ⓑ dense   Ⓓ humane

7. Most offices will not _____ frequent absences from work.

   Ⓐ attest   Ⓒ abide
   Ⓑ reinforce   Ⓓ impede

8. A security guard must be _____ and observant at all times.

   Ⓐ vigilant   Ⓒ habitual
   Ⓑ verbal   Ⓓ superficial

9. If you think you have not been treated fairly, seek _____ firmly but politely.

   Ⓐ admittance   Ⓒ infractions
   Ⓑ vaccine   Ⓓ redress

10. The actor was deeply insulted by the _____ comments about his performance.

    Ⓐ humane   Ⓒ sensible
    Ⓑ derogatory   Ⓓ prudent

11. Water poured through the _____ in the basement wall.

    Ⓐ malady   Ⓒ breach
    Ⓑ characteristic   Ⓓ novice

12. Ginger's car seems to _____ in wet weather.

    Ⓐ surrender   Ⓒ agitate
    Ⓑ strive   Ⓓ malfunction

GO ON ➡

Check the Spelling

Fill in the circle next to the word that is spelled correctly and best completes each sentence.

13. People who are _____ about safety put fellow workers at risk.

    Ⓐ lacts   Ⓒ lax
    Ⓑ laks   Ⓓ laxes

14. The issue caused _____ in the political party.

    Ⓐ dessension   Ⓒ disenssion
    Ⓑ dissension   Ⓓ dissenssion

15. The coach made an _____ choice in appointing the captains.

    Ⓐ arbitrary   Ⓒ arbatrary
    Ⓑ arbitrery   Ⓓ arbetrary

16. Technology has made space travel _____.

    Ⓐ feasible   Ⓒ feasable
    Ⓑ feesible   Ⓓ fiesible

17. Creditors may not _____ people who owe them money.

    Ⓐ harras   Ⓒ hurass
    Ⓑ harass   Ⓓ hirass

18. Don't _____ an idea until you try it.

    Ⓐ dismiss   Ⓒ dissmis
    Ⓑ dissmiss   Ⓓ dismis

19. Julie will try to _____ how many people are coming to the meeting.

    Ⓐ ascertain   Ⓒ ascirtane
    Ⓑ asertane   Ⓓ ascurtane

20. Planning a large meeting requires _____ attention to detail.

    Ⓐ meticuluos   Ⓒ meticulous
    Ⓑ maticuloss   Ⓓ maticulous

21. A _____ worker is a company's most important asset.

    Ⓐ raliable   Ⓒ ralaible
    Ⓑ reliable   Ⓓ reliabel

22. Many problems can be resolved with a little imagination and _____.

    Ⓐ initeative   Ⓒ initative
    Ⓑ inishiative   Ⓓ initiative

23. Someone with an _____ talent for math could be a good bookkeeper.

    Ⓐ inharent   Ⓒ inherent
    Ⓑ inherint   Ⓓ inharint

24. A job counselor can help people _____ their strengths and weaknesses.

    Ⓐ asess   Ⓒ assese
    Ⓑ assess   Ⓓ ases

STOP

Score: _____ / 24

Getting Help

Ⓐ Check the Meaning

Read the paragraphs below. Think about the meaning of the words in bold type.

Everyone needs a little help from time to time. One source of help is the state or local government. These governments have many programs and services that help people in the event of a **misfortune**, such as a fire or flood, or when unemployment makes day-to-day expenses a problem. Some programs are designed to **alleviate** housing problems by providing temporary shelter. Other agencies **counsel** people on money and budget problems. In some cases, the government may form an **alliance** with a local charity or a similar **benevolent** group to provide the needed assistance. The important thing is that those who need help reach someone **capable** of helping them.

How does one begin? Many of these programs are listed in the phone book under "Social and Human Services" or under the name of the city or state.

A visit to the agency office may **demoralize** some people. The process may seem impersonal and completely **devoid** of warmth and cheerfulness. People must answer a number of questions about their problems. This should not cause **dismay.** There is no hidden **motive** for such questions. They are simply a way of learning how best to address the problem.

An applicant will probably not know if he or she is **eligible** for assistance for days or weeks. A social worker will need to check and evaluate all information. A **subsequent** visit will sometimes be necessary to clarify information or to review the problem. Throughout the process, patience is required.

Check the Meaning

Choose the correct meaning for the word in bold type. Fill in the circle next to the correct meaning.

1. Another word for **eligible** is
   - (A) qualified.
   - (B) important.
   - (C) elevated.
   - (D) lengthy.

2. To **alleviate** is to
   - (A) rise up.
   - (B) relieve.
   - (C) rent.
   - (D) charge money.

3. An **alliance** is
   - (A) a team or partnership.
   - (B) everyone in the office.
   - (C) a government.
   - (D) a statement that is not true.

4. To **demoralize** is to
   - (A) preach a sermon.
   - (B) excite.
   - (C) send away.
   - (D) discourage.

5. Another word for **benevolent** is
   - (A) kind.
   - (B) boring.
   - (C) angry.
   - (D) thoughtless.

6. Another word for **subsequent** is
   - (A) earlier.
   - (B) twin.
   - (C) lower.
   - (D) later.

7. To **counsel** is to
   - (A) protect.
   - (B) arrest.
   - (C) advise.
   - (D) cure.

8. A **misfortune** is
   - (A) a large amount of money.
   - (B) something bad that happens.
   - (C) a type of help.
   - (D) a type of fire.

9. Another word for **motive** is
   - (A) movement.
   - (B) job.
   - (C) worker.
   - (D) reason.

10. People who are **devoid** of something
    - (A) are completely without it.
    - (B) do not need it.
    - (C) cannot find it.
    - (D) value it highly.

11. Another word for **dismay** is
    - (A) death.
    - (B) laughter.
    - (C) enjoyment.
    - (D) dread.

12. Another word for **capable** is
    - (A) intelligent.
    - (B) able.
    - (C) injured.
    - (D) simple.

Score: ___ / 12

B Study the Spelling

Word List

alleviate	capable	subsequent	motive	devoid	misfortune
counsel	eligible	demoralize	alliance	dismay	benevolent

Write the list word or words for each clue.

1. They end with *ble.* _____ _____

2. They end with *ent.* _____ _____

3. They have the same double consonant in their spelling.

_____ _____

4. They begin with the *de-* prefix.

_____ _____

5. This two-syllable word has the word *may* in its spelling.

_____

6. It has the same prefix as *miscount* and *mistrust.* _____

7. It has two syllables. The first syllable has four letters. _____

Add the missing syllable. Write the list word.

8. sub_____quent _____

9. eli_____ble _____

10. be_____olent _____

11. de_____ _____

12. alle_____ate _____

One word in each group is misspelled. Circle the misspelled word. Then write it correctly.

13. counsel   subsequent   motiv   _____

14. benevolent   demorelize   alleviate   _____

15. dissmay   motive   devoid   _____

16. capable   alliance   misforchune   _____

C Build Your Skills

Language Tutor

Some words sound alike, but they do not share the same spelling or meaning.
Study the meaning of the underlined words in these sentences.

The owners sought the <u>counsel</u> of the workers. The workers will <u>counsel</u> them to keep the plant open.

The president has a <u>council</u> of military advisors.

The dessert was the perfect <u>complement</u> to a great dinner.

The host got many <u>compliments</u> on the meal.

I had to <u>alter</u> my plans at the last minute.

The bride and groom walked slowly toward the <u>altar</u>.

Write the sentence. Add the correct word from within the parentheses.

1. My daughter was elected to the student (counsel; council) at her school.

_____

2. A colorful hat will (complement; compliment) your new dress.

_____

3. Will these reading glasses (altar; alter) my appearance?

_____

4. The teacher (complemented; complimented) me on my work.

_____

5. Jake (counseled; counciled) me to apply for the job.

_____

6. Members of the church covered the (altar; alter) with flowers.

_____

Score: ⬜/6

Ⓓ Proofread and Write

Donna wrote the following information when she applied for help from the government. She made four spelling mistakes. Cross out the misspelled words. Write the correct spellings above them.

Application for Assistance

Describe the problem: On Tuesday I learned to my dismay that the

landlord had not paid the electric bill, and the electricity was cut off. I

called him immediately and on several subsaquent occasions, but he

does not return my calls. I am not capable of paying the bill myself, and I

cannot afford to move to another apartment. My neighbor counsiled me.

She thought I might be eligable for some housing assistance until this

problem is cleared up. This would alleviate my problem. This misfortune

has demorilized me greatly.

Describe a problem you have had, or make up a problem, and ask for some type of assistance. Use at least four list words.

_____

_____

_____

_____

_____

_____

 Writing Portfolio

Proofread your description carefully and correct any mistakes. Then make a clean copy and put it in your writing portfolio.

Vacation Time

A Check the Meaning

Read the paragraphs below. Think about the meaning of the words in bold type.

No matter how busy you are, plan some vacation time each year. It does not have to be a **conventional** two-week trip. In fact, if time or money is tight, you may not want to **indulge** in a long or expensive trip. Instead, take a short trip that costs very little.

Think carefully about what you want. If you want to **savor** the peace and quiet of a beautiful natural spot, you do not need to rent a cabin by a **picturesque** lake. Instead, you might camp in a nearby national park. This way, you could enjoy a **placid** few days without spending a lot. Theme parks are a popular attraction. A trip to such a park can be quite expensive. To get the most for your money, avoid staying at a **luxurious** hotel. After all, you will spend most of the time elsewhere.

Choose the correct meaning for the word in bold type. Fill in the circle next to the correct meaning.

1. Another word for **picturesque** is
   - Ⓐ strange.
   - Ⓑ framed.
   - Ⓒ photographed.
   - Ⓓ beautiful.

2. If something is **luxurious**, it is
   - Ⓐ clean.
   - Ⓑ comfortable.
   - Ⓒ well-known.
   - Ⓓ empty.

3. When people **indulge** in something, they
   - Ⓐ take pleasure in it.
   - Ⓑ earn money at it.
   - Ⓒ dislike it.
   - Ⓓ avoid it.

4. **Placid** means
   - Ⓐ placed in a certain spot.
   - Ⓑ unreal or unbelievable.
   - Ⓒ full.
   - Ⓓ quiet or peaceful.

5. If something is **conventional**, it is
   - Ⓐ out of the way.
   - Ⓑ easy to use.
   - Ⓒ ordinary.
   - Ⓓ busy.

6. To **savor** is to
   - Ⓐ keep.
   - Ⓑ lose.
   - Ⓒ survive.
   - Ⓓ enjoy.

Check the Meaning

Have you ever wanted to rent a vacation home? If you like to **linger** over ads for mountain cabins or beach cottages, here are some tips.

Do not limit your search to just the popular locations. The ones that appear often in ads are usually expensive, so only the most **affluent** families can afford them. The ads may tell about the extras that are provided. However, be sure to ask about the more **mundane** things you use each day. For example, ask if glasses, cooking utensils, and towels are provided. Make sure, too, that the location will suit you. A **secluded** cabin may be too far from the things you need. Ask for a picture of the home, but remember that pictures can be misleading. A charming house on the outside may be uncomfortable inside, while a **nondescript** cottage can be quite cozy. Finding the perfect vacation home may seem like a difficult job at first, but a little planning can make your goal less **elusive**.

Choose the correct meaning for the word in bold type. Fill in the circle next to the correct meaning.

7. If something is **secluded**, it is
- (A) second in line.
- (B) away from other things.
- (C) in town.
- (D) in pieces.

8. Another word for **mundane** is
- (A) useful.
- (B) expensive.
- (C) steel.
- (D) common.

9. If something is **elusive**, it is
- (A) hard to get rid of.
- (B) expensive.
- (C) hard to get or to describe.
- (D) pictured.

10. If something is **nondescript**, it is
- (A) strong.
- (B) plain.
- (C) strange.
- (D) tall.

11. To **linger** is to
- (A) become scared.
- (B) stay a while.
- (C) laugh.
- (D) pass or skip.

12. Another word for **affluent** is
- (A) quiet.
- (B) strong.
- (C) cheap.
- (D) wealthy.

B Study the Spelling

indulge	placid	nondescript	affluent	picturesque	mundane
linger	savor	conventional	elusive	luxurious	secluded

Write the list word for each clue.

1. It is formed from the word *luxury*. _____

2. It rhymes with *favor*. _____

3. The first syllable is the prefix *non-*. _____

4. There is a double consonant in its spelling. _____

5. It ends with *ed*. _____

6. It has both the *-ion* and *-al* suffixes. _____

7. It rhymes with *finger*. _____

8. It begins like *indent* and ends like *bulge*. _____

Form a list word by matching the beginning of a word in the first column with its ending in the second column. Write the list word.

mun	ger	**9.** _____
plac	dane	**10.** _____
in	vor	**11.** _____
lin	id	**12.** _____
sa	dulge	**13.** _____

Add the missing letters. Write a list word.

14. nond___scri___t _____

15. lux___ri___us _____

16. conven___ion___l _____

17. pictures___ ___e _____

18. a___fl___ent _____

C Build Your Skills

A business letter has six main parts: a heading, an inside address, a greeting, a body, a closing, and a signature. Study the example on the next page. Note that a comma separates the date from the year and the city from the state. The envelope also has a special form. The envelope below goes with the letter on the next page.

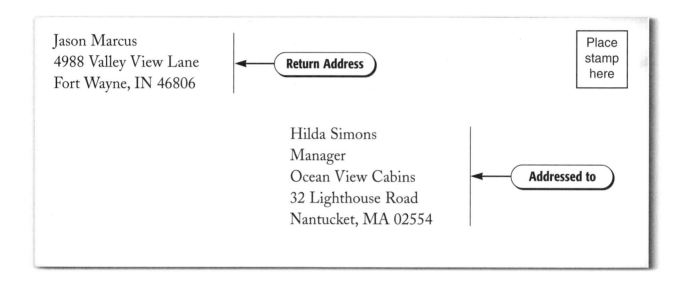

Study the envelope and the letter on the next page. Then answer these questions.

1. To whom is this letter being sent? _____

2. Who is sending this letter? _____

3. What is Hilda Simons' title? _____

4. What is the name of her business? _____

5. In what state is her business located? _____

6. What kind of punctuation is between the city and the state? _____

7. What kind of punctuation follows the greeting in the letter?

_____

8. What kind of punctuation follows the closing in the letter? _____

9. Is there a comma before the ZIP code? _____

10. In what part of the letter do you find the date? _____

11. Is the ZIP code on the same line as the city and state? _____

12. In what city and state does Mr. Marcus live? _____

Score: /12

Ⓓ Proofread and Write

Jason Marcus wrote this letter to get information about renting a vacation cabin. He made four spelling mistakes. Cross out the misspelled words. Write the correct spellings above them.

4988 Valley View Lane
Fort Wayne, IN 46806
February 17, 1997

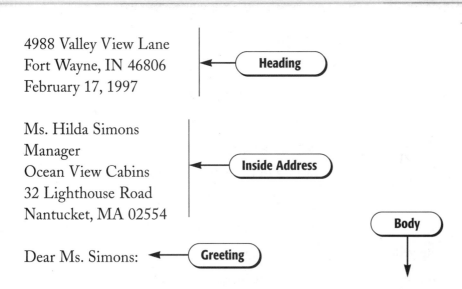

Ms. Hilda Simons
Manager
Ocean View Cabins
32 Lighthouse Road
Nantucket, MA 02554

Dear Ms. Simons: ◄── **Greeting**

    My family and I are interested in renting a vacation cabin for a week this summer and would appreciate getting some information on Ocean View Cabins. We prefer a secluded location with a pitchuresque view of the ocean where we can saver the saltwater breezes. We are mainly interested in escaping the mundain surroundings of the city and finding a place where we can indulge in hours of reading and fishing.

    My family and I do not require luxerious surroundings. However, we would like the conventional features of indoor plumbing and electricity.

    Please send information on your cabins as soon as possible. Include information on the rates, any necessary deposits, and the furnishings included with each cabin.

Sincerely yours, ◄── **Closing**

Jason Marcus ◄── **Signature**

Jason Marcus

 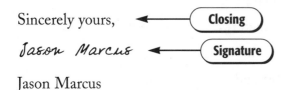

Writing Portfolio

Write a letter to a business and ask for some information. Use your own paper. Your letter might concern a vacation or some other product or service. Use at least four list words.

Proofread your letter carefully and correct any mistakes. Then make a clean copy to mail to the business or put in your writing portfolio.

Using the Telephone

A Check the Meaning

Read the paragraphs below. Think about the meaning of the words in bold type.

The telephone is something of a scientific miracle. Pressing the right buttons can put you in touch with nearly anyone in the world. However, knowing how to use a telephone directory is a **prerequisite** for using the telephone. A telephone directory contains a section of business listings and a section of **residential** listings. Residential listings are arranged alphabetically according to the resident's **surname**. To get the number of someone in another state, call an operator. In **metropolitan** areas, there is often a separate book for business listings. Commonly called the yellow pages, these pages group businesses according to type and then list the individual businesses alphabetically. Finding a particular business can be a **formidable** challenge if you are not sure where to look. When you need a place to stay, do you look under hotels, motels, or inns? Unless such listings are cross referenced, you may end up flipping page after page to no **avail**. Finding what you want can be a **tedious** chore. Luckily, most telephone directories include cross references.

Much of the time people spend on the telephone involves simple conversations about **trite** matters that have no purpose except a diversion from their daily routines. However, there are times when it is vitally important to give complete and accurate information. In an emergency, for example, you must be **coherent** and organized about what you say. Indicate the nature of the emergency and all **relevant** facts, such as the location. Leave out the **sundry** details that are **extraneous** to the problem at hand, as they will only confuse matters or waste time. Most important, do not hang up until you are told to do so. Staying on the line allows the operator to get additional information.

Check the Meaning

Choose the correct meaning for the word in bold type. Fill in the circle next to the correct meaning.

1. A **trite** matter is one that is
- (A) common and uninteresting.
- (B) funny or cute.
- (C) difficult to describe.
- (D) related to sports.

2. Another word for **tedious** is
- (A) joyful.
- (B) informative.
- (C) tiring.
- (D) expensive.

3. If something is **formidable**, it is
- (A) entertaining.
- (B) busy.
- (C) hard to overcome.
- (D) far away.

4. Another word for **relevant** is
- (A) telephone.
- (B) related.
- (C) easy.
- (D) obvious.

5. If something is **coherent**, it is
- (A) friendly and likable.
- (B) knowledgeable.
- (C) understandable.
- (D) stable.

6. If you work to no **avail**, your work is
- (A) of little value or use.
- (B) quickly forgotten.
- (C) rewarded.
- (D) finished early.

7. Another word for **sundry** is
- (A) necessary.
- (B) unpredictable.
- (C) cozy.
- (D) various.

8. If something is **extraneous**, it is
- (A) damaged beyond repair.
- (B) out of control.
- (C) not where it belongs.
- (D) irrelevant.

9. A **prerequisite** is
- (A) a type of math problem.
- (B) something needed beforehand.
- (C) a source of sorrow.
- (D) a type of machinery.

10. A **metropolitan** area is one that
- (A) is located on a foreign continent.
- (B) contains an important city.
- (C) has old-fashioned residents.
- (D) is in New York.

11. A **surname** is a
- (A) measure of importance.
- (B) medical procedure.
- (C) family name.
- (D) name of a business.

12. **Residential** means
- (A) having to do with homes.
- (B) land given to Native Americans.
- (C) similar in appearance.
- (D) informal.

B Study the Spelling

Word List

tedious	trite	formidable	extraneous	coherent	sundry
surname	avail	metropolitan	residential	prerequisite	relevant

Write the list word or words for each clue.

1. It has one syllable and begins with two consonants. _____

2. The word *sun* is part of its spelling. _____

3. They have two syllables and three vowels.

   _____   _____

4. It is formed from the word *resident*. _____

5. They end with the *-ous* suffix.

   _____   _____

6. The word *name* is part of its spelling. _____

7. It is formed from the word *metropolis*. _____

8. It begins like *relegate* and ends like *servant*. _____

9. The words *form* and *able* are part of its spelling. _____

10. They have four syllables and begin with a consonant. _____

    _____   _____

Write the list words with three syllables in alphabetical order. Use dots between the syllables.

11. _____   13. _____

12. _____   14. _____

Write the list word that comes between these words in the dictionary.

15. thought _____ tumble

16. superb _____ sustain

17. awesome _____ demonstrate

18. domestic _____ finger

Ⓒ Build Your Skills

Language Tutor

Suffixes can add meaning to a word or root. They can also change how a word is used. The following suffixes change naming or action words into describing words. If the naming or action word ends in *y*, change the *y* to *i* before adding the suffix.

Action or Naming Word	Suffix	Describing Word
a resident	-ial	a *residential* neighborhood
a marvel	-ous	a *marvelous* accomplishment
to study	-ous	a *studious* man
to trace	-able	a *traceable* crime
to laugh	-able	a *laughable* idea

Write the following sentences. Add a suffix to the underlined naming or action word in the first sentence to make it a describing word. Add the describing word to the second sentence.

1. The business began to <u>prosper</u>. It was soon a _____ business.

_____

2. Amy will <u>study</u> for hours every night. She is a _____ person.

_____

3. If Jason could <u>market</u> his ideas, he would be successful. Everyone says his ideas are _____.

_____

4. Natalie's wedding <u>ceremony</u> was very organized. She is quite skilled at planning _____ functions.

_____

5. The judge decided to <u>accept</u> the new evidence. She ruled it _____.

_____

6. Do not <u>rely</u> on Leticia to help you. She is not a _____ person.

_____

Score: ☐ / 6

Ⓓ Proofread and Write

Julio took the following notes during a meeting at work. He made four spelling mistakes. Cross out the misspelled words. Write the correct spellings above them.

Training Session Notes

Our delivery service faces a formidible task in the next few months. Holiday packages will be going to every residential neighborhood in the entire metropolitan area. It will be important to check the surname on each package very carefully. It will be a tedius task, but one that must be done very carefully.

No amount of speed will help drivers who do not know their routes. It may seem trite, but keep a street map in your truck. It can be the most relavent piece of equipment you have.

 Writing Portfolio

Think back to a meeting you attended at work, in school, or elsewhere. Make some notes on what you heard at that meeting. Use your own paper. Use at least four list words.

Proofread your notes carefully and correct any mistakes. Then make a clean copy and put it in your writing portfolio.

Respecting Others

(A) Check the Meaning

Read the paragraph below. Think about the meaning of the words in bold type.

The United States is not the **homogeneous** melting pot it once was. Today it is a rich mixture of **ethnic** groups, languages, customs, religions, and values. Because of this variety, tolerance and understanding are more important than ever. This means not only being **hospitable** to people who are different; it means attempting to learn and appreciate the **heritage** of others. New generations of immigrants import new holidays, customs, and values that may seem unusual or even **contradictory** to our more familiar ways of acting. What do Mexican Americans celebrate on May 5, or Cinco de Mayo? Why do some Jewish men and boys wear yarmulkes? Where did the festival of Kwanzaa originate? These customs help people **sustain** links to their ethnic, religious, and cultural traditions. Perhaps instead of a melting pot, America is a tossed salad.

Choose the correct meaning for the word in bold type. Fill in the circle next to the correct meaning.

1. If something is **homogeneous**, it is
(A) very intelligent.
(B) made up of similar parts.
(C) of historic importance.
(D) useful.

2. Another word for **heritage** is
(A) community.
(B) tradition.
(C) home.
(D) peace.

3. Another word for **contradictory** is
(A) opposite.
(B) pleasing.
(C) costly.
(D) strange.

4. To **sustain** is to
(A) disappoint.
(B) obey.
(C) change.
(D) keep alive.

5. If you are **hospitable**, you
(A) speak more than one language.
(B) celebrate different holidays.
(C) welcome others.
(D) give up easily.

6. An **ethnic** group
(A) is supported by the government.
(B) has high standards of behavior.
(C) shares a racial, religious, or cultural background.
(D) is found only in North America.

Check the Meaning

Read the paragraphs below. Think about the meaning of the words in bold type.

Some nations have an official state religion. People who are not members of that religion may be forced to support the state religion through their taxes. In extreme cases the government may even **deprive** such "nonbelievers" of certain rights.

Many of the earliest settlers came to this country to **secure** the right to practice religion freely without government **interference**. This did not necessarily mean they were tolerant of other faiths. In fact, our early history is full of examples of **treacherous** acts that the **prevalent** religious group **perpetrated** on smaller religious gatherings, such as the Quakers. The Bill of Rights was intended to end such injustice and allow all citizens the right to practice their religion without interference from the government or from others. That freedom applies not just to Quakers but to Hindus, Buddhists, Muslims, and people of all faiths.

Choose the correct meaning for the word in bold type. Fill in the circle next to the correct meaning.

7. Interference is
- Ⓐ a period of time.
- Ⓑ a popular religion.
- Ⓒ getting in the way of something.
- Ⓓ asking a series of questions.

8. To **secure** is to
- Ⓐ reduce in size.
- Ⓑ allow entry.
- Ⓒ draw or sketch.
- Ⓓ make certain or guarantee.

9. To **deprive** is to
- Ⓐ move quickly.
- Ⓑ take away.
- Ⓒ examine closely.
- Ⓓ fall into.

10. If something is **prevalent**, it is
- Ⓐ a source of happiness.
- Ⓑ often mistaken for something else.
- Ⓒ early.
- Ⓓ widespread or common.

11. A **treacherous** act is
- Ⓐ patriotic.
- Ⓑ kind and loving.
- Ⓒ disloyal and deceitful.
- Ⓓ carefully planned.

12. To **perpetrate** is to
- Ⓐ commit or do.
- Ⓑ brag repeatedly.
- Ⓒ enter forcefully.
- Ⓓ persuade.

B Study the Spelling

Word List

deprive	sustain	homogeneous	interference	hospitable	perpetrate
ethnic	secure	contradictory	treacherous	prevalent	heritage

Write the list word that is formed from each of these words.

1. treachery _____

2. contradict _____

3. prevail _____

4. interfere _____

5. hospitality _____

6. homogeneity _____

Write the list word or words for each clue.

7. It begins with the *pre-* prefix and has three syllables. _____

8. It has two syllables and three consecutive consonants. _____

9. It has two syllables and rhymes with *pain*. _____

10. It has three syllables. The second syllable is *i*. _____

11. It has three syllables. Two syllables begin with *p*. _____

12. They end with the *-ous* suffix. _____   _____

Write the words with two syllables. Use a dot between the syllables.

13. _____   15. _____

14. _____   16. _____

Add the missing syllable. Write the list word.

17. de_____   _____

18. _____nic   _____

19. heri_____   _____

20. hospi_____ble   _____

Score: ◻/20

C Build Your Skills

Language Tutor

The *inter-* prefix adds the meaning "between" or "among" to a word or root.

> interfere: to come between; to hinder.
>> Do not interfere with my plans.

The *intra-* prefix adds the meaning "within" to a word or root.

> intrastate: within the boundaries of a state.
>> The company sent us an intrastate shipment of lumber.

The underlined words in the following sentences have the *inter-* or *intra-* prefix. Think about the meaning and then write a brief definition for each underlined word.

1. The doctor injected the medicine into the patient's bloodstream using an <u>intravenous</u> device.

_____

2. The FBI was able to <u>intercept</u> the illegal shipment of exotic animals before it reached its destination.

_____

3. The Boston Red Sox and New York Yankees have a strong <u>intercity</u> rivalry.

_____

4. Belview High School has four teams in its <u>intramural</u> basketball league.

_____

5. A priest and a rabbi conducted the <u>interfaith</u> marriage ceremony.

_____

6. An <u>intercontinental</u> missile fired from Europe could reach North America.

_____

7. The university sent the book to my local library through an <u>interlibrary</u> loan.

_____

8. The first <u>intragalactic</u> trip will probably begin on Earth and end on Mars.

_____

D Proofread and Write

Bill wrote the following feature article about a cultural festival held in his city. He made four spelling mistakes. Cross out the misspelled words. Write the correct spellings above them.

City Celebrates Its Heratige

"America the Hospitable" was the theme for the weekend festival. Every ethnik group was represented in costume, food, and music. It was anything but a homogeneous gathering. Even a brief shower could not deprive participants from sharing the prevailent mood of laughter and harmony. In her closing remarks, Mayor Shapiro expressed the hope that everyone would sustane the spirit of this gathering in their day-to-day living. Only then, she said, could we all secure the American dream.

Write a short article on an event in your city or town that brought people together. Use at least four list words.

_____

_____

_____

_____

_____

_____

Writing Portfolio

Proofread your report carefully and correct any mistakes. Then make a clean copy and put it in your writing portfolio.

Unit 4 Review

Finish the Meaning

Fill in the circle next to the word that best completes each sentence.

1. The new tax is certain to have _____ opponents.

   Ⓐ relevant   Ⓒ humane

   Ⓑ formidable   Ⓓ arbitrary

2. Gloom was the _____ mood in the losing team's locker room.

   Ⓐ benevolent   Ⓒ prevalent

   Ⓑ frail   Ⓓ erratic

3. The senator's arguments were logical and _____.

   Ⓐ coherent   Ⓒ eligible

   Ⓑ mutual   Ⓓ dense

4. Two days of rain helped to _____ the long drought.

   Ⓐ indulge   Ⓒ entice

   Ⓑ alleviate   Ⓓ contaminate

5. Her disappointing speech was nothing more than a series of _____ comments.

   Ⓐ hospitable   Ⓒ invaluable

   Ⓑ fundamental   Ⓓ trite

6. The _____ pitcher can throw a baseball more than ninety miles per hour.

   Ⓐ capable   Ⓒ emotional

   Ⓑ mundane   Ⓓ superficial

7. Ed wanted to be married on the beach, but Sue preferred a _____ wedding.

   Ⓐ metropolitan   Ⓒ conventional

   Ⓑ verbose   Ⓓ definitive

8. Her purse is always filled with papers, coins, and other _____ items.

   Ⓐ secluded   Ⓒ subtle

   Ⓑ sundry   Ⓓ habitual

9. The police escorted the rock star so that he could get through the crowd without _____.

   Ⓐ interference   Ⓒ depression

   Ⓑ dismay   Ⓓ persistence

10. The vacation cottage overlooked a smooth, _____ lake.

    Ⓐ lax   Ⓒ generic

    Ⓑ moderate   Ⓓ placid

11. The runner could not _____ her early speed and finished last.

    Ⓐ secure   Ⓒ forfeit

    Ⓑ sustain   Ⓓ postpone

12. His _____ for starting the business was simple: he wanted to make money.

    Ⓐ maneuver   Ⓒ motive

    Ⓑ misfortune   Ⓓ anxiety

Check the Spelling

Fill in the circle next to the word that is spelled correctly and best completes each sentence.

13. Save money by avoiding _____ expenses.

- Ⓐ extraneuos
- Ⓒ ekstraneous
- Ⓑ extraneous
- Ⓓ extraenous

14. The storms caused _____ flooding.

- Ⓐ subsequent
- Ⓒ subsaquint
- Ⓑ subsaquent
- Ⓓ subsiquent

15. Poverty should never _____ a child of an education.

- Ⓐ depriv
- Ⓒ deprive
- Ⓑ diprive
- Ⓓ deprieve

16. The manager received _____ information on the problem.

- Ⓐ contradictary
- Ⓒ contradictery
- Ⓑ contrudictory
- Ⓓ contradictory

17. The police finally captured the _____ thief.

- Ⓐ ellusive
- Ⓒ eloosive
- Ⓑ elusave
- Ⓓ elusive

18. Seek the _____ of an expert before buying an antique.

- Ⓐ councel
- Ⓒ counsle
- Ⓑ counsel
- Ⓓ cownsel

19. Monica lives in a _____ apartment.

- Ⓐ luxurius
- Ⓒ luxurious
- Ⓑ luxureous
- Ⓓ luckurious

20. The lawyer insisted his client did not _____ the crime.

- Ⓐ purpetrate
- Ⓒ perpatrate
- Ⓑ perpetrate
- Ⓓ perpitrate

21. Meg hated the _____ job of marking price tags.

- Ⓐ tedious
- Ⓒ tediuos
- Ⓑ tedeous
- Ⓓ tedeus

22. The families in this community formed an _____ to fight crime.

- Ⓐ alliance
- Ⓒ aliance
- Ⓑ allience
- Ⓓ allianse

23. The _____ village was photographed frequently.

- Ⓐ picturesk
- Ⓒ picturesque
- Ⓑ picheresque
- Ⓓ pictureseque

24. Jazz is part of the American musical _____.

- Ⓐ heritage
- Ⓒ heritege
- Ⓑ heratage
- Ⓓ haritage

Score: _____ / 24

Review

99

UNIT 5: Government and Law

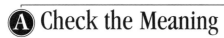

17 Money Matters

A Check the Meaning

Read the paragraphs below. Think about the meaning of the words in bold type.

It has been called the grim science; but grim or not, **economics**, the study of money, goods, and services, is important to everyone. Many people study American economics because the United States is a very **prosperous** country. It has a high standard of living, good roads, secure borders, and assistance for the needy. The money for these services comes from the wealth generated by its citizens. Part of that wealth goes to the government **treasury** through taxes. If the treasury runs out of money, it must **replenish** its supply of money through taxes or borrowing.

The government can **levy** taxes in many ways. Everyone earning a paycheck pays an income tax. The tax is usually deducted from a worker's **remuneration** and sent directly to the government. Every business pays a tax on the profit it makes. A **lucrative** business, one that makes a great deal of money, must pay higher taxes.

The money spent by people and businesses is an important **component** of the economy. Money spent on food, clothing, or new business equipment allows other people to have jobs. More **frugal** individuals may prefer to save their money. Deposits to a bank account may become a loan for someone to start a new business. In addition, the bank pays the saver interest. Money used in this way to make more money is called **capital**.

People also use money to start or expand a business. One way to own part of a company is to buy its stock. As an **investor**, you share in the profits and in any losses. Unlike most savings accounts, investing in a business is risky. Many people find the risks **exorbitant**, so only those who know something about a business should buy its stock.

100 **Unit 5:** Government and Law

Check the Meaning

Choose the correct meaning for the word in bold type. Fill in the circle next to the correct meaning.

1. If something is **exorbitant**, it is
   A) cheap and ordinary.
   B) boring.
   C) great or extreme.
   D) busy.

2. To **replenish** is to
   A) lose.
   B) shine.
   C) reply.
   D) refill.

3. A **treasury** is a
   A) place that keeps money.
   B) geometric figure.
   C) person who pays bills.
   D) wealthy person.

4. Another word for **remuneration** is
   A) figures.
   B) payment.
   C) fractions.
   D) work.

5. **Economics** is
   A) a place where money can be saved for the future.
   B) the water and air around us.
   C) the study of money, goods, and services.
   D) a type of news program.

6. An **investor** is someone who
   A) is a type of detective.
   B) buys part of a company or property.
   C) refuses to pay taxes.
   D) has a high standard of living.

7. Another word for **component** is
   A) comment.
   B) compliment.
   C) part.
   D) wealth.

8. **Capital** is
   A) an important building.
   B) money used to make more money.
   C) money spent foolishly.
   D) part of a bank.

9. A **prosperous** country or business
   A) has little money.
   B) is very large.
   C) is for sale.
   D) does very well.

10. A **frugal** person
   A) does not waste money.
   B) does not trust banks.
   C) hides money.
   D) earns a lot of money.

11. A **lucrative** business is one that
   A) uses money from the government.
   B) invests in other businesses.
   C) does not pay taxes.
   D) earns a lot of money.

12. To **levy** is to
   A) collect or charge.
   B) buy.
   C) ignore for a long time.
   D) wait for more information.

Score: ___/12

B Study the Spelling

Word List

remuneration	economics	component	prosperous	frugal	treasury
replenish	capital	levy	investor	lucrative	exorbitant

Write the list word or words for each clue.

1. They begin with *re*. _____ _____

2. Change the last letter of *treasure* to make this word. _____

3. The word *prosper* is part of this word. _____

4. It has four letters and two syllables. _____

5. They end with *al*. _____ _____

6. The word *orbit* is part of its spelling. _____

7. It ends with the *-or* suffix, meaning "one who." _____

8. It is formed from the word *economy*. _____

9. It has three syllables and ends with *ent*. _____

10. It has three syllables and ends with *tive*. _____

Add the first or last syllable. Write a list word.

11. replen_____ _____

12. _____vestor _____

13. _____ury _____

14. _____crative _____

15. exorbi_____ _____

16. _____gal _____

One word in each group is misspelled. Circle the misspelled word, then write it correctly.

17. economics   componant   frugal   _____

18. levey   lucrative   exorbitant   _____

19. replenish   treasury   remunuration   _____

20. prosperus   capital   investor   _____

C Build Your Skills

Language Tutor

Add 's to singular words to make them show ownership or possession.

Add just an apostrophe (') to plural words that end in *s* to make them show ownership or possession. If the plural does not end in *s*, add 's.

Singular Possessive	**Plural Possessive**
the investor's money	the citizens' concerns
a child's toy	the children's playground

Rewrite each sentence. Change the underlined words to make them show ownership or possession.

1. The accountant helped prepare <u>the tax return of my parents.</u>

_____

2. Few students understood <u>the answer of the teacher.</u>

_____

3. A spokesperson explained <u>the demands of the workers.</u>

_____

4. A letter was delivered to <u>the mailbox of Norma.</u>

_____

5. <u>Hats for women</u> are sold on the second floor.

_____

6. The meeting was held in <u>the office of her boss.</u>

_____

7. The <u>loud roars of the lions</u> could be heard in the jungle.

_____

8. The trail led to <u>the edge of the river.</u>

_____

Ⓓ Proofread and Write

Christine planned to start a painting and wallpapering business. Before meeting with a business advisor, she wrote some questions. Christine made four spelling mistakes. Cross out the misspelled words. Write the correct spellings above them.

Questions to Ask My Advisor

- I have $5,000 to invest in my new business. Is this enough capital?

- Would it be wise to get another invester for this business?

- A newspaper ad will cost $400. Is this an exorbitant price?

- I will need to hire some help for big jobs. What kind of renumeration would be fair?

- Does the state levy a tax on my truck?

- How often should I replensh my supply of wallpapers?

- Is it realistic to expect to have a prosprous business in two years?

Write some questions you have about a business you would like to own. Use your own paper. Use at least four list words.

Writing Portfolio

Proofread your questions carefully and correct any mistakes. Then make a clean copy and put it in your writing portfolio.

Looking at History

Ⓐ Check the Meaning

Read the paragraph below. Think about the meaning of the words in bold type.

The history of a war, it is said, is always written by the winner. In other words, when you read history, you should remember who wrote it. The way you perceive an event depends on who you are and how you see things. Historians are no different. How they **portray** events will reflect their particular points of view. Writers in other times may look at events differently. A good example of a historical **controversy** is the differing views of the westward expansion of the United States. Were the pioneers brave explorers who brought freedom and order to a **chaotic** land, or were they thieves who tried to **seize** tribal lands from Native Americans? The attitude toward this **epoch** in American history has changed—not because the events have changed, but because we see these events differently. How **posterity** sees the past will depend largely on who reports it. This fact may have caused automobile pioneer Henry Ford to say, "History is bunk."

Choose the correct meaning for the word in bold type. Fill in the circle next to the correct meaning.

1. Posterity is
- Ⓐ a group of historians.
- Ⓑ the past.
- Ⓒ a type of building.
- Ⓓ future generations of people.

2. A **controversy** is a
- Ⓐ disagreement.
- Ⓑ swimming contest.
- Ⓒ historic event.
- Ⓓ pioneer.

3. If something is **chaotic**, it is
- Ⓐ modern.
- Ⓑ attractive.
- Ⓒ confused.
- Ⓓ musical.

4. To **portray** is to
- Ⓐ carry.
- Ⓑ lie.
- Ⓒ describe.
- Ⓓ hide.

5. Another word for **seize** is
- Ⓐ take.
- Ⓑ cut.
- Ⓒ beg.
- Ⓓ view.

6. An **epoch** is
- Ⓐ a type of medicine.
- Ⓑ a short summary.
- Ⓒ an area set aside for special use.
- Ⓓ a period of time.

Check the Meaning

Read the paragraph below. Think about the meaning of the words in bold type.

Our sense of history does not come only from history textbooks. It also comes from fictional accounts in novels and movies. Such stories often provide a different **version** of events to suit a story. For decades fiction portrayed slavery as an **idyllic** life full of music, good health, and generous slave owners. Nothing, of course, could have been further from the truth. In reality, enslaved people were **subjugated** through cruel punishments and were forced to live in poverty. Only the strongest could endure such **adversity**. Often ignored were the **insurgents** who revolted against the system or escaped to the North. Even after Lincoln **emancipated** the people who were enslaved, life for African Americans was extremely difficult. Slavery, like many unpleasant facts of our history, can be difficult to face, but it helps us understand who we are.

Choose the correct meaning for the word in bold type. Fill in the circle next to the correct meaning.

7. To **subjugate** is to
- (A) understand.
- (B) subdue or conquer.
- (C) judge or decide.
- (D) enjoy.

8. An **idyllic** life is
- (A) lazy.
- (B) one that is found in the South.
- (C) very short.
- (D) simple and easy.

9. Another word for **adversity** is
- (A) success.
- (B) freedom.
- (C) escape.
- (D) hardship.

10. To **emancipate** is to
- (A) set free.
- (B) employ.
- (C) neglect.
- (D) praise.

11. A **version** is
- (A) a type of poetry.
- (B) a description from one point of view.
- (C) an imaginary event.
- (D) the highest point in an area.

12. An **insurgent** is a
- (A) rebel.
- (B) military officer.
- (C) writer.
- (D) troublesome child.

Score: /12

B Study the Spelling

Word List

portray	version	controversy	chaotic	adversity	emancipate
seize	subjugate	epoch	idyllic	posterity	insurgent

Write the list word or words for each clue.

1. It violates the rule, "*i* before *e* except after *c*." _____

2. There is a double consonant in its spelling. _____

3. It is formed from the word *adverse*. _____

4. They end with the adjective suffix *-ic*.

_____ _____

5. It ends with a *k* sound that is spelled *ch*. _____

6. It begins like *verbal* and ends like *session*. _____

Write the list word used to make these words.

7. insurgency _____

8. emancipation _____

9. controversial _____

10. subjugation _____

11. portrayal _____

12. seizure _____

Add the missing letters. Write the list word.

13. post___r___ty _____

14. ins___rg___nt _____

15. cha___t___c _____

16. adv___r___ity _____

17. ___poc___ _____

18. ver___ ___on _____

19. p___rtra___ _____

20. eman___ ___pate _____

C Build Your Skills

Language Tutor

The *ad-* prefix adds the meaning "toward" or "near" to a root. The meaning of the root, however, is often no longer apparent.

The spelling of the *ad-* prefix changes when it is added to roots that begin with *c, f, g, k, l, p, q, s,* and *t*. The result usually is a double consonant spelling. Study these examples.

ad-	+	cident	=	accident		ad-	+	firm	=	affirm
ad-	+	gravate	=	aggravate		ad-	+	low	=	allow
ad-	+	pear	=	appear		ad-	+	sess	=	assess

Add the prefix and roots below to make other words. Change the spelling of the prefix when necessary.

1. ad- + curate   =   _____

2. ad- + semble   =   _____

3. ad- + fection   =   _____

4. ad- + cord   =   _____

5. ad- + prove   =   _____

6. ad- + set   =   _____

7. ad- + count   =   _____

8. ad- + flict   =   _____

9. ad- + point   =   _____

10. ad- + gressive   =   _____

11. ad- + legation   =   _____

12. ad- + cent   =   _____

13. ad- + signment   =   _____

14. ad- + sociate   =   _____

15. ad- + fix   =   _____

⒟ Proofread and Write

Maria took the following notes in her history class. She made four spelling mistakes. Cross out the misspelled words. Write the correct spellings above them.

The slavery question caused great controversy in

nineteenth-century America. When the Civil War began,

few in the North wanted to emancapate the slaves.

The South tried to portray slavery as necessary to

its economy and beneficial for the enslaved people.

Freeing these people, it claimed, would cause a

chaodic situation. Many in the North accepted this

version of slavery or chose to ignore the problem.

Eventually this issue led to the bloodiest epock of our

country's history. Race relations are far from perfect.

However, posterity will never again permit one race to

so cruelly subjagate another.

Read about or recall a time in the past. On another piece of paper, write a brief summary of your understanding of the events. Use at least four list words.

Writing Portfolio

Proofread your summary carefully and correct any mistakes. Then make a clean copy and put it in your writing portfolio.

The Right to Vote

Ⓐ Check the Meaning

Read the paragraphs below. Think about the meaning of the words in bold type.

The idea that ordinary men and women should have the right to vote is rarely questioned today. This was not always the case in the United States. Although the framers of the U.S. Constitution often **affirmed** their belief in the equality of all people, their actions suggested otherwise. In the early years of our nation, the **electorate** was limited to white males who owned land or possessed great wealth. It took nearly a hundred years before the Fifteenth Amendment to the Constitution made it illegal to deny someone the right to vote because of race. Even then, some communities found ways to **obstruct** this right. In some cases a poll tax was levied on voters. In others a "literacy" test was required and graded by biased officials. Such taxes and tests were merely a **ruse** to deny poor people or African Americans the right to vote. Voting rights would **embroil** the United States in a bitter controversy during the 1960s. It took the Twenty-fourth Amendment to end poll taxes. Later President Lyndon Johnson **proposed**, and Congress passed, the Voting Rights Act of 1965, which outlawed literacy tests.

Women also had to fight for the right to vote. They began in 1848, but it was 1920 before the **franchise** was extended to women. For decades, the movement had few supporters. Bills to grant women the vote were defeated year after year. Protests, demonstrations, letters, and similar **tactics** were used to **vie** for the necessary votes. Finally, in 1918, President Woodrow Wilson changed his mind and became an **ally** of the cause. Even after the president **endorsed** an amendment giving women the right to vote, Congress **adjourned** without approving it. It took two years and a special session of Congress before it passed.

Check the Meaning

Choose the correct meaning for the word in bold type. Fill in the circle next to the correct meaning.

1. Another word for **ruse** is
- (A) entertainment.
- (B) race.
- (C) trick.
- (D) explanation.

2. The **electorate** is
- (A) an unfair tax.
- (B) anyone living in a city.
- (C) information for voters.
- (D) the voting population.

3. To **embroil** is to
- (A) cook over a flame.
- (B) throw into confusion.
- (C) lose interest in something.
- (D) fold together.

4. An **ally** is a
- (A) political party.
- (B) supporter.
- (C) recorder.
- (D) government official.

5. If you **affirm** a belief, you
- (A) declare it to be true.
- (B) pass a law about it.
- (C) give reasons for it.
- (D) change it frequently.

6. To **vie** is to
- (A) care little about.
- (B) compete.
- (C) count.
- (D) study carefully.

7. Another word for **tactic** is
- (A) method.
- (B) money.
- (C) joke.
- (D) appointment.

8. To **obstruct** is to
- (A) improve.
- (B) give away.
- (C) get in the way of.
- (D) instruct.

9. To **adjourn** is to
- (A) rebel.
- (B) stop for a time.
- (C) submit to a law.
- (D) change slightly.

10. A **franchise** is
- (A) a type of clothing.
- (B) part of the Constitution.
- (C) harsh criticism.
- (D) the right to vote.

11. To **endorse** is to
- (A) repeat.
- (B) adjust.
- (C) support.
- (D) complain.

12. To **propose** is to
- (A) suggest.
- (B) upset.
- (C) force.
- (D) apply.

B Study the Spelling

Word List

ruse	franchise	propose	affirm	electorate	tactic
endorse	ally	vie	obstruct	embroil	adjourn

Write the list word or words for each clue.

1. They have a double consonant in their spelling.

_____   _____

2. They begin with the *ad-* prefix. The spelling of the prefix changes in one of the words.

_____   _____

3. It is formed from the word *elect*. _____

4. It begins like *embrace* and rhymes with *soil*. _____

5. Add a suffix to this word to make *alliance*. _____

6. They begin with two consonants.

_____   _____

7. They have two syllables. Both syllables begin with the same consonant.

_____   _____

8. They have just one syllable.

_____   _____

Write the list word that is part of these words.

9. obstruction _____

10. endorsement _____

11. adjournment _____

Add the missing syllable. Write the list word.

12. em_____   _____

13. elec_____ate   _____

14. ob_____   _____

C Build Your Skills

Language Tutor

A comma separates three or more items in a series. The items can be words or groups of words.
Place the comma after each item except the last one.

Protests, demonstrations, and letters were used to vie for the necessary votes.
　　1　　　　2　　　　3

Voters could be discouraged by levying poll taxes, demanding literacy tests,
　　　　　　　　　　　　　　　　1　　　　　　　　2

and threatening anyone who tried to vote.
　　　　3

Write these sentences. Add commas where they are needed. Not all sentences will need commas.

1. People have been discriminated against because of their race religion or sex.

_____

2. It took generations before women African Americans and the poor were able to vote.

_____

3. People sought support in businesses on farms and in schools.

_____

4. The law was passed and sent to the President in two days.

_____

5. Aaron stepped into the booth closed the curtain and cast his vote.

_____

6. The struggle was long and bitter, but they finally won.

_____

7. The candidate was frowning biting her lip and wringing her hands as she waited
for the election results.

_____

8. Always register early study the issues and vote for your beliefs.

_____

Score: ☐/8

Ⓓ Proofread and Write

Kwan wrote the following letter to his senator. He made three spelling mistakes. He also forgot to use two commas. Cross out the misspelled words. Write the correct spellings above them. Add the commas where they belong.

4559 South Essex St.

Saginaw, MI 48606

August 19, 1997

Senator Harlan Oates

Senate Office Building

Washington, D.C. 20510

Dear Senator Oates:

As a member of the electorate, I am asking you to afirm your support of Senate Bill 599, the Animal Rights Act. Anyone who studies this bill will endorse what it is attempting to do. Yet year after year, its few opponents manage to obstuck its passage with lies misinformation and similar tactics. Last year a legal ruse was used to keep it from even coming to a vote. Please do not allow Congress to adjern without approving this bill.

Sincerely,

Kwan Lee

Kwan Lee

Writing Portfolio

Write a letter to one of your representatives in Congress. Use your own paper. Ask your representative to support or oppose a particular bill. Use at least four list words.

Proofread your letter carefully and correct any mistakes. Then make a clean copy to mail to your representative or put in your writing portfolio.

The Courts and the Law

A Check the Meaning

Read the paragraph below. Think about the meaning of the words in bold type.

Unlike most government officials, judges usually keep their jobs for a long time, even for life. There is a reason for this. Judges' decisions to offer **leniency** and **rehabilitation** or punishment should be based on the law and how it applies to the individual. Most judges do not have to engage in the **partisan** politics of an election to keep their jobs. Therefore, decisions can be based on what is right rather than on what is popular. An **influential** businessperson and an **obscure** laborer should be treated the same in the eyes of the law. Whether judges can do so is a matter of opinion. Some people feel that the rich can **circumvent** the aim of the law by hiring expensive lawyers. Without such legal assistance, someone may be more likely to be found guilty. It is, therefore, also the job of the judge to see that certain basic rights of the accused, such as the right to a lawyer, are protected.

Choose the correct meaning for the word in bold type. Fill in the circle next to the correct meaning.

1. Leniency is
Ⓐ a tendency to lean.
Ⓑ gloominess.
Ⓒ a type of illness.
Ⓓ gentleness or mercy.

2. If someone is **obscure**, he or she is
Ⓐ not well known.
Ⓑ impure.
Ⓒ well liked.
Ⓓ highly educated.

3. To **circumvent** is to
Ⓐ allow air to flow through.
Ⓑ defeat or go around.
Ⓒ cut into small pieces.
Ⓓ draw a circle around.

4. Partisan means
Ⓐ broken into parts.
Ⓑ lawless.
Ⓒ loyal to a political party or cause.
Ⓓ logical and sound.

5. An **influential** person
Ⓐ has studied the law.
Ⓑ is clever with words.
Ⓒ rarely changes his or her mind.
Ⓓ has power over others.

6. Rehabilitation is
Ⓐ an opportunity to regain one's good name or status.
Ⓑ where prisoners are kept.
Ⓒ a relative.
Ⓓ a long explanation.

Check the Meaning

Besides upholding the law, the courts interpret the laws of the land. What do words like *freedom* and *equality* really mean? Laws are made up of such words. As legislatures create more and more laws, the courts must **construe** what these laws mean. The courts can also look at **antiquated** laws and review their meanings in a changing world. For more than 100 years an equal education for African American and white children meant **segregated** schools. However, in 1954 the Supreme Court changed its position and decided separate schools were by their nature **inferior** schools. It decided to **rescind** all state laws that forced African American children into separate schools. One strength of the U.S. Constitution is that it can be changed and interpreted in new ways by different generations. This **resilience** allows us to admit the errors of the past and adapt our laws to new understandings.

Choose the correct meaning for the word in bold type. Fill in the circle next to the correct meaning.

7. To **construe** is to
- (A) turn away.
- (B) explain.
- (C) confuse.
- (D) use up.

8. Resilience is
- (A) an important question.
- (B) a weakness.
- (C) the ability to recover.
- (D) a feeling of disgust.

9. To **rescind** is to
- (A) restore.
- (B) delay.
- (C) strengthen.
- (D) cancel.

10. If something is **segregated**, it is
- (A) taken away suddenly.
- (B) moved from place to place.
- (C) separated from others.
- (D) often seen in public.

11. An **inferior** school is one that is
- (A) lower in quality.
- (B) greatly admired.
- (C) run by a religious group.
- (D) expensive to operate.

12. Antiquated means
- (A) expensive.
- (B) too old to be useful.
- (C) predictable.
- (D) energetic.

Score: / 12

B Study the Spelling

Word List

segregated	leniency	rescind	antiquated	influential	circumvent
inferior	partisan	construe	obscure	resilience	rehabilitation

Write the list word that is formed from each of these words.

1. lenient _____

2. resilient _____

3. rehabilitate _____

4. influence _____

Write the list word or words for each clue.

5. It begins like *circumstance* and ends like *prevent*. _____

6. They have an *ie* in their spelling.

_____   _____

7. They begin with the *in-* prefix.

_____   _____

8. The word *cure* is part of its spelling. _____

9. It has two syllables. The first syllable is the *re-* prefix. _____

10. The word *true* is part of its spelling. _____

11. There is a *qu* in its spelling. _____

12. They have three syllables.

_____   _____

Add the missing syllable. Write the list word.

13. con_____   _____

14. seg_____gated   _____

15. an_____quated   _____

16. ob_____   _____

17. inferi_____   _____

18. reha_____itation   _____

C Build Your Skills

Language Tutor

The Latin word for *circle* is *circus*. This Latin word is the source of the prefix *circum-*, meaning "around" or "about."

    circumvent   to go around, surround, or avoid

The Latin word for *across* or *beyond* is *trans*. This Latin word is the source of the prefix *trans-*, meaning "across," "through," or "beyond."

    transport   to carry from one place to another

There is still a trace of the Latin meaning in English words with these prefixes.

Read the sentences below. Think about the meaning of the underlined word. Then write a short definition of the word.

1. A fence around the <u>circumference</u> of the field kept the cows from escaping.

_____

2. We gave blood in case Jennifer needed a <u>transfusion</u> after her operation.

_____

3. I sometimes <u>transpose</u> the *i* and the *e* when spelling the word *seize*.

_____

4. The candidate was a master of <u>circumlocution</u>; he never gave us a direct answer.

_____

5. In 1522 one of Magellan's ships completed the first <u>circumnavigation</u> of the globe.

_____

6. Youth is a <u>transient</u> time in one's life and should be enjoyed while it lasts.

_____

7. George was in a difficult <u>circumstance</u>; he was caught in traffic and late for work.

_____

8. Snow will <u>transform</u> a plain landscape into a picturesque scene.

_____

                        Score: / 8

Ⓓ Proofread and Write

Ali wrote this draft for a report in his citizenship class. He made four spelling errors. Cross out the misspelled words. Write the correct spellings above them.

The Dred Scott Case

In an obscure courthouse in St. Louis, Missouri, one of the worst judicial decisions in history was made. In the 1850s, slavery was a highly partisun issue. To circumvent making a final decision about slavery, some states were allowed to join the Union as free states and some as slave states. The practice of slavery created great divisions in the country. Eventually the courts had to constrew what this meant for an enslaved man named Dred Scott, whose owner took him from a slave state to a free state. Chief Justice Roger Taney decided that an enslaved person was the property of his or her owner, even in free states. This made the African American inferier to the white population in the eyes of the law. It took the Civil War and several amendments to the Constitution to resind the Dred Scott decision.

Writing Portfolio

Write a short report on something to do with the law or the courts. Use your own paper. You may wish to check a reference book such as an encyclopedia or draw on your own experiences. Use at least four list words.

Proofread your report carefully and correct any mistakes. Then make a clean copy and put it in your writing portfolio.

Unit 5 Review

Finish the Meaning

Fill in the circle next to the word that best completes each sentence.

1. I exercised my _____ by voting for Penny Armstrong.

   Ⓐ anxiety   Ⓒ franchise
   Ⓑ resilience   Ⓓ legislation

2. He registered his car in another state in an attempt to _____ the sales tax.

   Ⓐ circumvent   Ⓒ forfeit
   Ⓑ degrade   Ⓓ retrieve

3. We paid less for our clothes, but we got an _____ brand.

   Ⓐ exorbitant   Ⓒ expedient
   Ⓑ inferior   Ⓓ adjacent

4. Her call was just a _____ to get me to her house for my surprise party.

   Ⓐ transfusion   Ⓒ remuneration
   Ⓑ complication   Ⓓ ruse

5. Trees _____ my view of the ocean.

   Ⓐ procure   Ⓒ agitate
   Ⓑ obstruct   Ⓓ contaminate

6. I was not sure how to _____ the look he gave me.

   Ⓐ confirm   Ⓒ construe
   Ⓑ entice   Ⓓ affirm

7. The army tried to _____ the rebellious citizens.

   Ⓐ subjugate   Ⓒ inoculate
   Ⓑ emancipate   Ⓓ procure

8. Most great men and women have had to overcome some _____ in their lives.

   Ⓐ endeavor   Ⓒ component
   Ⓑ tactic   Ⓓ adversity

9. After the storm, stores began to charge _____ prices for ice and batteries.

   Ⓐ reliable   Ⓒ exorbitant
   Ⓑ oblivious   Ⓓ verbose

10. We put a newspaper and several photographs in a time capsule for _____.

    Ⓐ diversion   Ⓒ circumstance
    Ⓑ initiative   Ⓓ posterity

11. After the cold weather, we had to _____ the oil in the car's engine.

    Ⓐ replenish   Ⓒ undermine
    Ⓑ embroil   Ⓓ savor

12. The witness's _____ of what happened differed from that of the police.

    Ⓐ refrain   Ⓒ version
    Ⓑ transaction   Ⓓ breach

Check the Spelling

Choose the word that is spelled correctly and best completes each sentence.

13. Jane Addams, an _____ of the poor, sought better conditions for factory workers.

Ⓐ allie   Ⓒ ally
Ⓑ alye   Ⓓ aleye

14. Renting bicycles in resort areas can be a very _____ business.

Ⓐ lucrative   Ⓒ lucrutive
Ⓑ lucretive   Ⓓ lucrateve

15. My uncle holds an _____ job in the mayor's office.

Ⓐ influintial   Ⓒ influencial
Ⓑ inflewential   Ⓓ influential

16. With four children, my kitchen is quite _____ in the morning.

Ⓐ chayotic   Ⓒ kaotic
Ⓑ chaotic   Ⓓ chaotec

17. This business will need some _____ to get started.

Ⓐ capatle   Ⓒ kapital
Ⓑ capital   Ⓓ capatol

18. The committee decided to _____ at midnight.

Ⓐ ajern   Ⓒ ajurn
Ⓑ adjern   Ⓓ adjourn

19. Country living seems quite _____ until you think about all the work.

Ⓐ idyllic   Ⓒ idillic
Ⓑ idylic   Ⓓ idilick

20. Some governments temporarily _____ certain civil liberties during wartime.

Ⓐ rascind   Ⓒ rescind
Ⓑ rassind   Ⓓ rescend

21. We expect at least seven companies to _____ for the contract to rapair the roads.

Ⓐ vigh   Ⓒ vye
Ⓑ veye   Ⓓ vie

22. The proposed law created much _____ among the voters.

Ⓐ controversie   Ⓒ controversy
Ⓑ contraversey   Ⓓ contraversy

23. Every party member voted along _____ lines and rejected the bill.

Ⓐ partisan   Ⓒ partisun
Ⓑ partisen   Ⓓ partasen

24. An increase in dues will add needed funds to the union's _____.

Ⓐ treazury   Ⓒ treasery
Ⓑ treasury   Ⓓ traesury

STOP

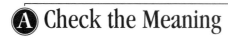

21 Examination Preparation

Ⓐ Check the Meaning

Read the paragraphs below. Think about the meaning of the words in bold type.

Everyone expects to take examinations while in school. It is an established part of an **academic** setting. However, schools are not the only **institutions** that test people. States often test nurses, electricians, truck drivers, and many others before granting them licenses to do their work. These exams cover more than the mere **rudiments**. In fact, they can be quite **comprehensive**. As a result, such licensing exams can be rather **voluminous**, consisting of many pages and taking hours to complete.

If you plan to take an important test like the ones described above, ask the testing agency to provide a sample test. It will help you decide which areas of study are **pertinent** to the test. Most licensing exams focus on the **terminology** used in a job. Flash cards are a good way to study this vocabulary. To make a flash card, write a word on one side of an index card and the definition on the other. Study the card. Then look at the word and write its meaning. Finally, close your eyes and try to **visualize** the word in your mind.

Do not try to learn everything you need to know in one sitting. Your **retention** will be much greater if you study for an hour each day rather than for seven hours in one day. If you study several books or articles to prepare for the test, write a brief summary of the material to **facilitate** your learning. You can also use this **synopsis** to review the material just before the test.

Look over the entire test before you begin. Answer the questions you are sure of first. Then you will know how much time you have left to **ponder** the more difficult questions. Try to leave yourself time to check your answers before turning in the test.

Check the Meaning

Choose the correct meaning for the word in bold type. Fill in the circle next to the correct meaning.

1. To **ponder** is to
   - (A) turn around.
   - (B) leave behind.
   - (C) send ahead.
   - (D) think over.

2. The **terminology** of a field is its
   - (A) computer software.
   - (B) special words.
   - (C) equipment.
   - (D) managers.

3. If something is **voluminous**, it is
   - (A) quite large.
   - (B) unimportant.
   - (C) an imitation.
   - (D) very old.

4. If something is **pertinent**, it is
   - (A) rude and hateful.
   - (B) unchanging over time.
   - (C) clear and easily understood.
   - (D) related to what is being considered.

5. To **visualize** is to
   - (A) move about rapidly.
   - (B) form a mental picture.
   - (C) speak in favor of.
   - (D) make a movie.

6. **Rudiments** are
   - (A) reddish colors.
   - (B) bad manners.
   - (C) basics.
   - (D) rules and regulations.

7. If something is **academic**, it is
   - (A) widespread.
   - (B) worthless.
   - (C) related to schools.
   - (D) harmful to one's health.

8. Another word for **synopsis** is
   - (A) explanation.
   - (B) literature.
   - (C) pride.
   - (D) summary.

9. Another word for **institution** is
   - (A) hospital.
   - (B) organization.
   - (C) school.
   - (D) church.

10. A **comprehensive** examination
    - (A) covers a broad range of material.
    - (B) is easy to understand.
    - (C) is given only by government agencies.
    - (D) determines how healthy one is.

11. To **facilitate** is to
    - (A) make easier.
    - (B) change one's mind frequently.
    - (C) hold someone's attention.
    - (D) slow down.

12. **Retention** is the ability to
    - (A) remain silent.
    - (B) find a job.
    - (C) hold or remember.
    - (D) wait patiently.

B Study the Spelling

Word List

ponder	rudiments	synopsis	institution	facilitate	comprehensive
pertinent	retention	academic	visualize	terminology	voluminous

Write the list word or words for each clue.

1. They have the *-ion* suffix.

_____   _____

2. It has two syllables and rhymes with *wander*. _____

3. It has four syllables. There are two *t*'s, two *a*'s, and two *i*'s in its spelling.

_____

4. It has three syllables. The vowel in the first syllable is *y*.

_____

5. It has three syllables and is plural. _____

6. It has five syllables. One syllable is *o*. _____

7. It is related to *comprehend*, meaning "to understand." _____

8. It begins like *pertain* and ends like *bent*. _____

Write the list words formed from these words.

9. volume _____

10. visual _____

11. academy _____

12. institute _____

13. retain _____

Add the missing letters. Write the list word.

14. compr___hens___ve _____

15. vi___uali___e _____

16. volum___n___us _____

17. pond___ ___ _____

18. s___nops___s _____

Build Your Skills

Language Tutor

The *-logy* suffix comes from the Greek word *logos*, meaning "word" or "speech." When used in English words, it usually adds the meaning "study" to a word or root.

term (words) + -logy (study) = terminology (the study of special words)

bio (life) + -logy (study) = biology (the study of life)

Each word in the box below has the *-logy* suffix. Write the word from the box next to its meaning.

ecology	mineralogy	geology	mythology
zoology	sociology	theology	physiology
bacteriology	psychology	criminology	technology

1. the study of animals and animal life _____

2. the scientific study of crime and criminals _____

3. the study of such things as coal, iron, and silver _____

4. the study of stories about gods and goddesses _____

5. the study of human society _____

6. the science of mental behavior _____

7. the study of God and religion _____

8. the study of living things and their environments _____

9. the study of certain small, one-celled organisms _____

10. the study of living things and how their bodies operate

_____

11. the study of mechanical and physical forces and how to control them

_____

12. the study of physical features of the earth _____

Ⓓ Proofread and Write

Juanita wrote the following letter to a community college asking for information on a course. She made four spelling mistakes. Cross out the misspelled words. Write the correct spellings above them.

2898 Belmont Avenue

Duluth, MN 55803

March 14, 1997

Director of Admissions

Roosevelt Community College

44 College Street

Duluth, MN 55802

Dear Director:

Please send me a catalog of courses offered by your institution for the fall semester. I would like to take a comprehensive, yet practical, course in writing. I am interested in one that covers the rudements of grammar without too much emphasis on accademic matters like terminology. A course that stressed writing a synopsis of voluminus reports would be particularly pertinant to my needs. I appreciate your sending me the catalog and making any recommendations on suitable courses.

Sincerely,

Juanita Ramos

Juanita Ramos

Writing Portfolio

Write a letter to a community college. Use your own paper. Ask for information on a course you would like to take. Use at least four list words.

Proofread your letter carefully and correct any mistakes. Then make a clean copy to mail or to put in your writing portfolio.

Learning on the Job

Ⓐ Check the Meaning

Read the paragraph below. Think about the meaning of the words in bold type.

Even the most **exemplary** employee receives an occasional **reproach** from his or her supervisor. Whether it is for some **blatant** violation of a work rule or a minor issue, criticism is always upsetting. The first reaction to criticism often is to defend your actions or reject the criticism as unfair or **erroneous**. This **spontaneous** response only **aggravates** the situation. If your supervisor feels you do not even acknowledge that you made a mistake, he or she will see no hope of your job performance improving. On the other hand, if you respond in a positive manner, criticism can have a positive outcome. For example, ask for clarification to be sure you understand the problem and admit to your mistake. If you show that you are committed to doing a better job, your supervisor will have more confidence in your work.

Choose the correct meaning for the word in bold type. Fill in the circle next to the correct meaning.

1. Another word for **blatant** is
- Ⓐ simple.
- Ⓑ unnecessary.
- Ⓒ obvious.
- Ⓓ small.

2. A **spontaneous** act is
- Ⓐ automatic or natural.
- Ⓑ selfish.
- Ⓒ done slowly and carefully.
- Ⓓ carried out secretly.

3. To **aggravate** something is to
- Ⓐ explore it.
- Ⓑ examine it.
- Ⓒ make it grow.
- Ⓓ make it worse.

4. An **exemplary** employee
- Ⓐ is an example to others.
- Ⓑ does not have to follow the rules.
- Ⓒ needs additional training.
- Ⓓ has many years of experience.

5. An **erroneous** statement
- Ⓐ is long and boring.
- Ⓑ contains errors.
- Ⓒ is spoken loudly.
- Ⓓ comes from an important person.

6. A **reproach** is
- Ⓐ a bonus.
- Ⓑ sorrow for a mistake.
- Ⓒ a second chance.
- Ⓓ blame or criticism.

Check the Meaning

Read the paragraph below. Think about the meaning of the words in bold type.

Experience is a good but sometimes cruel teacher. A new employee working alone is **apt** to make many mistakes before mastering a job. One way to **avert** these trials and errors is teaming a new worker with a **mentor,** an experienced worker who can give the beginner advice. If a new worker studies the habits and skills of a veteran, he or she may be able to **emulate** those habits and skills. More and more, employers are learning that such **collaboration** makes new workers feel more secure. It also is a way of recognizing the value of experienced workers. This teamwork approach is also being used in other ways. In some companies top executives meet with plant workers to share problems and seek solutions. Such meetings serve to **dispel** the belief that workers and managers cannot work together.

Choose the correct meaning for the word in bold type. Fill in the circle next to the correct meaning.

7. To **emulate** is to
- (A) reject.
- (B) copy.
- (C) decide.
- (D) empty.

8. A **mentor** is
- (A) a trusted adviser.
- (B) an enemy.
- (C) a merchant.
- (D) an unreliable worker.

9. To **avert** a problem is to
- (A) study it.
- (B) overlook it.
- (C) worry about it.
- (D) avoid it.

10. Another word for **apt** is
- (A) likely.
- (B) seldom.
- (C) hoping.
- (D) trying.

11. Collaboration is
- (A) a loud noise.
- (B) working together.
- (C) something that falls apart easily.
- (D) a sticky material.

12. To **dispel** is to
- (A) misspell.
- (B) make interesting.
- (C) drive away or scatter.
- (D) prove beyond a doubt.

B Study the Spelling

Word List

avert	exemplary	reproach	collaboration	blatant	dispel
erroneous	mentor	spontaneous	aggravate	apt	emulate

Write the list word or words for each clue.

1. They end with *ate*. _____ _____

2. It is formed from the word *collaborate*. _____

3. It has just one syllable. _____

4. They have a double consonant in their spelling. _____

_____ _____

5. It begins like *mental* and ends like *motor*. _____

6. It is formed from the word *example*. _____

7. It has two syllables. The second syllable has six letters. _____

8. They end with *ous*. _____ _____

9. It has two syllables. The first syllable has just one letter. _____

10. It has two syllables and begins with two consonants. _____

Write *avert, dispel, apt,* and *blatant* in alphabetical order. Use dots between the syllables.

11. _____

13. _____

12. _____

14. _____

Add the missing syllables. Write the list word.

15. spon_____ne_____ _____

16. _____labo_____tion _____

17. em_____ _____ _____

18. ex_____pla_____ _____

19. men_____ _____

20. re_____ _____

C Build Your Skills

Language Tutor

According to Greek mythology, Odysseus left his trusted friend and advisor, Mentor, in charge of his household during his long absences. It is from this story that we get the modern meaning of *mentor*, a trusted friend and advisor. This is just one example of an English word that began as a proper name.

Read each description below of a person or a place. Then complete the statement about the meaning of the underlined word.

1. A fair held in honor of St. Audrey sold cheap scarves and other cloth goods. The pronunciation of *Audrey* gradually changed to <u>tawdry</u>. Today, tawdry has come to mean _____

   _____

2. Charles Boycott was a landlord who charged high rents. He was so disliked that people decided to have nothing to do with him. Today if you <u>boycott</u> a business, you _____

   _____

3. The Hospital of Saint Mary of Bethlehem was a hospital for the mentally ill. It was a noisy and confused place. Bethlehem was often shortened to *Bedlam*. Now <u>bedlam</u> means _____

   _____

4. Jules Leotard was a French trapeze artist. He wore a tight-fitting, one-piece garment when he performed. Today a <u>leotard</u> is _____

   _____

5. Ambrose E. Burnside, a Union general during the Civil War, wore heavy side whiskers but shaved his chin. Today <u>sideburns</u> are _____

   _____

6. Franz Mesmer, an eighteenth-century doctor, used hypnosis to put his patients into a sleeplike state. Today the term <u>mesmerize</u> means _____

   _____

Score: __ / 6

Ⓓ Proofread and Write

The following memo appeared on the bulletin board where Paul works. The memo has four spelling mistakes. Cross out the misspelled words. Write the correct spellings above them.

MEMO

DATE: 9/12/97

TO: All Employees

FROM: Marita O'Brien

General Manager

A number of erroneous rumors have been reported about the future of this plant. To dispell these rumors, I want to make it clear that we plan to continue to do business at this location for many years. The ongoing collaberation between union representatives and management has allowed us to avurt a strike. Your exemplary dedication to solving our problems has been above reproach. It is something the entire industry might emmulate. I am proud of what we have accomplished and feel we are apt to continue such progress well into the future.

Writing Portfolio

Write a memo to a supervisor or another person where you work or would like to work. Use your own paper. Make suggestions for improvements or ask about the company's future. Use at least four list words.

Proofread your memo carefully and correct any mistakes. Then make a clean copy and send it or put it in your writing portfolio.

23 Presenting Information

Ⓐ Check the Meaning

Read the paragraphs below. Think about the meaning of the words in bold type.

Suppose you came across a note that read, "Ship sinks immediately." Would you send kitchen sinks to someone or would you ask how many lives were lost? **Ambiguous** messages like this one can be confusing. It is the sender's job to make messages as clear as possible for a reader to **discern**.

On and off the job, it is essential to communicate accurately with customers, fellow workers, and family members. The first step is to **formulate** a clear purpose for the message. Do not be content with some vague **concept** such as "to tell some stuff about safety." Be precise. What is the "stuff"? Is it a new piece of safety equipment, a scheduled fire drill, or improved protective gear? Once the purpose is established, do not **digress** from this purpose as you write. Every sentence may not deal with your subject directly, but your purpose should always be **implicit**.

Organizing your information is an **integral** part of a successful message. If you are giving directions for doing something, explain the steps in **chronological** order. Tell the reader what to do first, second, and so on. If you are describing something, the description might move from top to bottom or left to right. This way of organizing information is called **spatial** organization because it describes a certain space in a systematic way. More **abstract** topics require a different type of organization. If you want to convince someone of something, state your belief clearly. Then present several **plausible** reasons, one by one, for holding that belief. The **climax** of a message usually comes at the end since this is the part most readers remember. It is wise, therefore, to save your strongest reason for last.

Check the Meaning

Choose the correct meaning for the word in bold type. Fill in the circle next to the correct meaning.

1. To **formulate** is to
   - Ⓐ make serious and formal.
   - Ⓑ bring good luck.
   - Ⓒ plan in a careful way.
   - Ⓓ send forth.

2. If items are in **chronological** order, they
   - Ⓐ have been arranged quickly.
   - Ⓑ are in the order in which they occurred.
   - Ⓒ are in alphabetical order.
   - Ⓓ have been sorted by a computer.

3. To **discern** is to
   - Ⓐ see clearly.
   - Ⓑ show concern.
   - Ⓒ disown.
   - Ⓓ confuse.

4. Another word for **plausible** is
   - Ⓐ pleasant.
   - Ⓑ painful.
   - Ⓒ outrageous.
   - Ⓓ believable.

5. An **abstract** topic is
   - Ⓐ not made up of physical matter.
   - Ⓑ foolish.
   - Ⓒ easily explained.
   - Ⓓ related to art.

6. An **ambiguous** message
   - Ⓐ is short and to the point.
   - Ⓑ explains a problem.
   - Ⓒ can be understood in two ways.
   - Ⓓ lacks interest.

7. To **digress** is to
   - Ⓐ offer an opinion.
   - Ⓑ decide quickly.
   - Ⓒ break into parts.
   - Ⓓ depart from.

8. **Implicit** means
   - Ⓐ impolite.
   - Ⓑ meant, but not directly stated.
   - Ⓒ very simple.
   - Ⓓ progressing in small, planned steps.

9. The **climax** is
   - Ⓐ what remains after a fire.
   - Ⓑ a lengthy description.
   - Ⓒ a type of literature.
   - Ⓓ the point of highest interest.

10. **Spatial** means
    - Ⓐ having to do with space.
    - Ⓑ unfinished.
    - Ⓒ unable to make up one's mind.
    - Ⓓ richly decorated.

11. A **concept** is a
    - Ⓐ feeling of concern.
    - Ⓑ collection of stories.
    - Ⓒ general idea or understanding.
    - Ⓓ quiet period of time.

12. Another word for **integral** is
    - Ⓐ violent.
    - Ⓑ essential.
    - Ⓒ exciting.
    - Ⓓ numerous.

B Study the Spelling

Word List

spatial	ambiguous	chronological	discern	concept	integral
implicit	abstract	plausible	digress	formulate	climax

Write the list word contained in each of these words.

1. conceptual _____

2. digression _____

3. misconception _____

4. implicitly _____

5. anticlimax _____

6. implausible _____

Write the list word or words for each clue.

7. The word *logic* is part of its spelling. _____

8. It begins with two consonants and rhymes with *facial*. _____

9. It has four syllables. The third syllable is the vowel *u*. _____

10. Change the first three letters in *concern* to make this word.

   _____

11. They end with *al*. _____

   _____   _____

12. It ends with a double consonant. _____

13. It has three syllables. The vowel in each syllable is *i*. _____

14. It begins with a vowel and ends with two consonants. _____

One word in each group is misspelled. Circle the misspelled word, then write it correctly.

15. climax   intagral   concept   _____

16. ambigous   abstract   implicit   _____

17. plausable   formulate   spatial   _____

18. chronological concept   digres   _____

© Build Your Skills

Language Tutor

The Greek word for time is *khronos*. This is the source of the word part *chrono-* in English words. The Latin word for time is *tempus*. This is the source of the word part *tempo-* in English words. Both *chrono-* and *tempo-* add the meaning "time" to a word or root.

chronological	arranged according to time of occurrence
temporary	for a limited time

Each underlined word contains the word part *chrono-* or *tempo-*. Read each sentence and think about the meaning of the underlined word. Then write a short definition for it.

1. His <u>chronic</u> headaches made holding a steady job difficult. The pain distracted him for long periods of time. _____

   _____

2. I love the upbeat <u>tempo</u> of traditional jazz. It makes me want to tap my feet.

   _____

   _____

3. As word processors became popular, typewriters were soon an <u>anachronism</u> in most offices. _____

   _____

4. Henry David Thoreau and Ralph Waldo Emerson were <u>contemporaries</u>. Both lived in Concord, Massachusetts, and visited each other frequently. _____

   _____

   _____

5. The general knew he had to <u>synchronize</u> the movement of his armies to launch the attack on both fronts. _____

   _____

6. The captain kept a detailed <u>chronicle</u> of the voyage from beginning to end.

   _____

   _____

⒟ Proofread and Write

Below is a draft copy of a committee report. It contains four spelling mistakes. Cross out the misspelled words. Write the correct spellings above them.

Committee Report

As requested, this committee looked into the problems of the cooling system. There are several plausibal causes for the problem, but more tests will be needed before we can disern an exact cause. When the unit was installed, the workers may have ignored spatial requirements for such a system. Although the exact needs were left rather ambiguous, the need for extra room around the vent seemed implisit in the diagram. We suggest opening the vent area to see if that solves the problem. Since the cooling system is an integril part of our machinery, we should act immediately. With your approval, we will formulate a plan.

Writing Portfolio

Write a report on a problem you have studied at home or on the job. Use your own paper. Use at least four list words.

Proofread your report carefully and correct any mistakes. Make a clean copy and put it in your writing portfolio.

Overcoming Problems

(A) Check the Meaning

Read the paragraph below. Think about the meaning of the words in bold type.

Even experienced managers sometimes encounter problems they cannot solve alone. A manager who is in a **quandary** over some **perplexing** problem may benefit from discussing it with others, especially the workers closest to the problem. If goods are not getting to a destination on time, the manager might ask the dispatchers and drivers about the source of the delay. Perhaps the **discrepancy** between the scheduled time and the actual time is the result of traffic or road conditions. Sometimes a brief meeting with a few experienced and **perceptive** people will help a manager identify the problem and **devise** a solution. One person with limited information can only begin to **surmise** the cause of a problem; input from people with a variety of experiences can lead to a better understanding of it.

Choose the correct meaning for the word in bold type. Fill in the circle next to the correct meaning.

1. To **surmise** is to
   - (A) guess.
   - (B) look over.
   - (C) state.
   - (D) wonder.

2. Another word for **discrepancy** is
   - (A) compromise.
   - (B) change.
   - (C) consideration.
   - (D) difference.

3. A **perceptive** person is one who
   - (A) takes chances.
   - (B) likes meetings.
   - (C) is cooperative.
   - (D) has keen insight.

4. A **quandary** is
   - (A) a small room.
   - (B) a difficulty.
   - (C) an open rock pile.
   - (D) a disagreement.

5. To **devise** is to
   - (A) question.
   - (B) share.
   - (C) prepare.
   - (D) ignore.

6. Another word for **perplexing** is
   - (A) puzzling.
   - (B) old.
   - (C) common.
   - (D) unusual.

Check the Meaning

Read the paragraph below. Think about the meaning of the words in bold type.

Perhaps the most dangerous enemy of any organization is **apathy**. This **insidious** sense of indifference may go unnoticed to the casual manager, but it can cripple the workplace. Once it spreads through the work force, even the most dedicated people find it hard to **muster** the enthusiasm needed to do a job well. Before long, progress can come to a **virtual** standstill. When this happens, it is important to find a way to create a sense of pride in one's work and **optimism** about the future. The manager must help workers overcome the usual **inertia** when change is needed. One strategy is to help workers see how their specific jobs are important to the success of the company. Understanding the importance of one's work and getting praise for a job well done are the most important factors in worker morale. The smart supervisor gives praise often.

Choose the correct meaning for the word in bold type. Fill in the circle next to the correct meaning.

7. To **muster** is to
   - Ⓐ gather together or call up.
   - Ⓑ put behind.
   - Ⓒ criticize harshly.
   - Ⓓ injure.

8. **Apathy** means
   - Ⓐ happiness.
   - Ⓑ unusual behavior.
   - Ⓒ the desire to work quickly.
   - Ⓓ a lack of interest.

9. Someone who possesses **optimism**
   - Ⓐ shows respect for the property of others.
   - Ⓑ is well known in the community.
   - Ⓒ expects everything to turn out for the best.
   - Ⓓ is cruel and unjust.

10. **Insidious** means
   - Ⓐ insulting.
   - Ⓑ secretly harmful.
   - Ⓒ innocent of a crime.
   - Ⓓ open and honest.

11. Another word for **virtual** is
   - Ⓐ actual.
   - Ⓑ impossible.
   - Ⓒ easy.
   - Ⓓ imaginary.

12. **Inertia** is
   - Ⓐ a desire to travel.
   - Ⓑ a lack of self-respect.
   - Ⓒ an ability to avoid serious mistakes.
   - Ⓓ a tendency to resist change.

Score: ╱ 12

B Study the Spelling

Word List

quandary	muster	surmise	devise	discrepancy	optimism
perceptive	apathy	perplexing	virtual	insidious	inertia

Write the list word or words for each clue.

1. It is formed from the word *perceive*. _____

2. They begin with the *in-* prefix.

_____   _____

3. The vowel in their last syllable is *y*. _____

_____   _____

4. It begins like *virtue* and ends like *dual*. _____

5. They rhyme with *revise*. _____   _____

6. Change the vowel in the first syllable of *master* to make this word.

_____

7. It has the same second syllable as *complex*. _____

8. It has the same first syllable as *opposite*. _____

9. There are three *i*'s in its spelling. _____

10. It ends with two vowels. _____

Add the missing vowels. Write the list word.

11. opt___m___sm   _____

12. discr___p___ncy   _____

13. p___rplex___ng   _____

14. m___st___r   _____

15. v___rtu___l   _____

16. d___v___se   _____

C Build Your Skills

Language Tutor

The Greek word *an* means "without" or "not." It appears as the prefix *a-* or *an-* in English words.
The Greek word *pathos* means "feelings" or "suffering." It is the root of a number of English words.

a (without) + pathos (feelings) = apathy (without feelings)

The underlined word in each sentence contains either the *a-* prefix, the *an-* prefix, or the *pathos* root.
Study the word and the sentence. Then write a short definition for the underlined word.

1. The tornado destroyed everything in its path, proving once again that nature

is <u>amoral</u>. _____

_____

2. The <u>sympathy</u> of her friends helped Ida through the crisis. _____

_____

_____

3. After the government officials fled, the country was in a state of <u>anarchy</u>.

_____

_____

4. The pictures of the starving children were the most <u>pathetic</u> thing I have ever

seen. _____

_____

_____

5. Sleeping all night is <u>atypical</u> behavior for infants who are less than six months old.

_____

_____

6. The proposal to raise taxes again met with considerable <u>antipathy</u> among voters.

_____

_____

Score: /6

Ⓓ Proofread and Write

The following notes were placed in the suggestion box of a large company. The notes contain four spelling mistakes. Cross out the misspelled words. Write the correct spellings above them.

Worker apathy has become a serious problem in the machine shop. If management would devize a plan to pay a bonus for increased production, morale would improve.

I surmise that someone is spreading the insidius rumor that our health benefits will be ending soon. Please make an announcement to clear up this question.

It would be easy to muster some interest in a company softball team. Getting a team together in time for summer would be a virtual certainty.

The bookkeeping department is in a quandery over the discrepancy we find each month between our figures and those of the bank. An improved computer system would solve this preplexing problem.

Writing Portfolio

Write some suggestions for a suggestion box where you work or where you plan to work someday. Use your own paper. Use at least four list words.

Proofread your suggestions carefully and correct any mistakes. Then make clean copies and place them in a suggestion box or put them in your writing portfolio.

Unit 6 Review

Finish the Meaning

Fill in the circle next to the word that best completes each sentence.

1. There was a huge _____ between what the governor said and what she did.

   Ⓐ controversy Ⓒ discrepancy
   Ⓑ quandary Ⓓ synopsis

2. The candidate's remarks were followed by a _____ round of applause.

   Ⓐ perceptive Ⓒ virtual
   Ⓑ spontaneous Ⓓ comprehensive

3. Boston Latin School is one of the oldest _____ institutions in the nation.

   Ⓐ spatial Ⓒ academic
   Ⓑ partisan Ⓓ perceptive

4. Children tend to _____ the behavior of their parents.

   Ⓐ emulate Ⓒ muster
   Ⓑ avert Ⓓ rescind

5. The jury felt they had heard no _____ reason to convict him of the crime.

   Ⓐ insidious Ⓒ inferior
   Ⓑ obscure Ⓓ plausible

6. A sense of _____ among voters about the election led to a low voter turnout.

   Ⓐ ruse Ⓒ inertia
   Ⓑ apathy Ⓓ leniency

7. The captain had to _____ a plan to attack the enemy stronghold.

   Ⓐ circumvent Ⓒ construe
   Ⓑ devise Ⓓ digress

8. The jury was left to _____ the evidence without interruption.

   Ⓐ proliferate Ⓒ propose
   Ⓑ subjugate Ⓓ ponder

9. One cannot be a good writer without knowing the _____ of grammar.

   Ⓐ controversy Ⓒ rudiments
   Ⓑ epoch Ⓓ resilience

10. My father-in-law is not only my friend, he is my _____.

    Ⓐ mentor Ⓒ concept
    Ⓑ franchise Ⓓ insurgent

11. From the wreckage, experts were able to _____ several possible causes for the crash.

    Ⓐ emancipate Ⓒ surmise
    Ⓑ portray Ⓓ levy

12. Questions forced the teacher to _____ from her planned lecture.

    Ⓐ discern Ⓒ vie
    Ⓑ digress Ⓓ derive

GO ON

Check the Spelling

Fill in the circle next to the word that is spelled correctly and best completes each sentence.

13. The suspended player was guilty of a _____ violation of the rules.

- (A) blatent
- (B) blaitant
- (C) blatant
- (D) blatunt

14. There was an _____ report of a fire on Main Street.

- (A) erroneous
- (B) eroneous
- (C) erronious
- (D) erronnious

15. Renting a large truck will _____ moving our belonings.

- (A) fasilitate
- (B) facilatate
- (C) facilutate
- (D) facilitate

16. Do not _____ the dog while it is eating.

- (A) aggrivate
- (B) agravate
- (C) aggravait
- (D) aggravate

17. I hardly knew what to think of her _____ remark about my clothes.

- (A) ambiguous
- (B) ambigous
- (C) ambeguous
- (D) ambigueous

18. It took days to learn the _____ used in the computer manual.

- (A) turminology
- (B) terminologey
- (C) terminology
- (D) termanology

19. Try to _____ what the room will look like after it is painted.

- (A) vizualise
- (B) visualize
- (C) vishalize
- (D) visalize

20. List five historic events in _____ order.

- (A) chronlogical
- (B) chranalogical
- (C) chronological
- (D) chronolagical

21. The strong wind and tide should _____ the oil spill in the bay.

- (A) dispel
- (B) dispell
- (C) disspell
- (D) disspel

22. Capturing the fugitive required close _____ between the police and FBI.

- (A) collaboration
- (B) colaboration
- (C) collaberation
- (D) collaburation

23. The judge ruled the evidence _____ to the case.

- (A) pertinant
- (B) pertenent
- (C) pretenent
- (D) pertinent

24. Our task was to summarize the _____ report in less than a page.

- (A) voluminous
- (B) volumious
- (C) volumenus
- (D) volumanous

Score: _____ / 24

Post-test

Part 1: Meaning

For each item below, fill in the letter next to the word or phrase that most nearly expresses the meaning of the first word.

> **Sample**
>
> hammer
> - Ⓐ part of the arm
> - ⬤ a tool used for driving nails
> - Ⓒ a type of vegetable
> - Ⓓ to mix thoroughly

1. expedient
- Ⓐ excellent
- Ⓑ suitable for a particular purpose
- Ⓒ thoughtful and considerate
- Ⓓ generous

2. implicit
- Ⓐ damaged beyond repair
- Ⓑ exact
- Ⓒ suggested indirectly
- Ⓓ closely related

3. circumvent
- Ⓐ go around
- Ⓑ open wide
- Ⓒ hold back
- Ⓓ criticize angrily

4. chaotic
- Ⓐ careful
- Ⓑ clever
- Ⓒ false and misleading
- Ⓓ confused

5. tedious
- Ⓐ tiny
- Ⓑ curious
- Ⓒ tiresome
- Ⓓ often repeated

6. derogatory
- Ⓐ questionable
- Ⓑ unfavorable
- Ⓒ part of a laboratory
- Ⓓ energetic

7. oblivious
- Ⓐ unaware
- Ⓑ solemn and religious
- Ⓒ related to outer space
- Ⓓ scholarly

8. posterity
- Ⓐ posture
- Ⓑ predictions
- Ⓒ false reputation
- Ⓓ future generations

9. resilience
- Ⓐ natural surroundings
- Ⓑ type of container
- Ⓒ ability to recover
- Ⓓ inability to move about

10. synopsis
- Ⓐ an evil plot
- Ⓑ summary
- Ⓒ type of engraving
- Ⓓ someone devoted to art

GO ON ➡

Part 2: Spelling

For each item below, fill in the letter next to the correct spelling of the word.

11. (A) vigilant   (C) vigilent
    (B) vigalant   (D) vigulent

12. (A) afluent   (C) afluint
    (B) affluant   (D) affluent

13. (A) dispence   (C) dispense
    (B) dispens   (D) despense

14. (A) miscelaneous   (C) miscelleneous
    (B) miscellaneous   (D) mescellaneous

15. (A) leniency   (C) lenency
    (B) leneincy   (D) leniencey

16. (A) prevelent   (C) prevalent
    (B) previlent   (D) prevalant

17. (A) persistance   (C) persistense
    (B) presistence   (D) persistence

18. (A) scrutinize   (C) scrutenize
    (B) scrotinize   (D) scrutenise

19. (A) prospurous   (C) prosperus
    (B) prosperous   (D) prospirous

20. (A) treacherus   (C) treacherous
    (B) trecherous   (D) treachrous

21. (A) voluntary   (C) volintary
    (B) voluntery   (D) volentery

22. (A) disern   (C) dicern
    (B) dascern   (D) discern

23. (A) agravate   (C) aggrivate
    (B) aggravate   (D) agravate

24. (A) aliance   (C) allianse
    (B) allience   (D) alliance

25. (A) complacation   (C) complicasion
    (B) complication   (D) complecation

26. (A) deliberate   (C) daliberate
    (B) delibrate   (D) delliberate

27. (A) erroneus   (C) erroneous
    (B) eroneous   (D) erronious

28. (A) indispensible   (C) indispenzible
    (B) indaspensible   (D) indispensable

29. (A) impertanent   (C) impertinant
    (B) impertinent   (D) impurtinent

30. (A) impead   (C) impede
    (B) impeed   (D) impied

STOP

Score: ___ / 30

How to Use the Dictionary

Letters and symbols give the **pronunciation**. Use the pronunciation key to sound out the word.

The **part of speech** is given after the pronunciation.

The **definition** tells you the meaning. When there is more than one meaning, each meaning is numbered.

Each **word** is listed in alphabetical order and separated into syllables.

o·pen /ō′ pən/ −*adj.* **1.** Not closed; allowing passage in and out: *The cow got out of the pen through the open gate.* **2.** Available for business: *The store is open most evenings.* −*verb* To uncover or unwrap; to unfasten.

pen¹ /pĕn/ −*noun* A tool for writing.

Two different **words with the same spelling** are numbered.

pen² a fenced-in area, often used to keep animals.

Sometimes you will be told to look up a **simpler form** of the word.

ran /răn/ −*verb* The past form of *run*: *We ran to the bus stop.*

Other forms of the word are often shown.

Sometimes a **sample sentence** is given to make the definition clearer.

run /rŭn/ −*verb* **ran, running. 1.** To move quickly on foot: *Horses run faster than people.* **2.** To move around freely: *Don't let your pets run through the neighborhood.*

Pronunciation Key

ă	cat	ī	ice	o͞o	food	hw	which
ā	day	î	near	yo͞o	cute	zh	usual
â	care	ŏ	hot	o͝o	book	ə	about
ä	father	ō	go	ŭ	drum		open
ĕ	wet	ô	law	û	fur		pencil
ē	see	oi	oil	*th*	this		lemon
ĭ	pit	ou	out	th	thin		circus

Mini-Dictionary

a·bide /ə **bīd′**/ -*verb* **abode** or **abided, abiding, abides.** To put up with; allow: *Teachers will not abide students cheating on tests.*

ab·nor·mal /ăb **nôr′** məl/ -*adj.* Not normal, usual, or average; unusual: *The cold temperatures in the summer were abnormal.*

ab·stract /ăb **străkt′**/ or /**ăb′** străkt/ -*adj.* **1.** Expressing a quality that is not made up of physical matter: *Love is an abstract idea.* **2.** Hard to understand.

ac·a·dem·ic /ăk′ ə **dĕm′** ĭk/ -*adj.* Relating to schools: *Although the academic studies were difficult, they were interesting.*

ac·cel·er·ate /ăk **sĕl′** ə rāt′/ -*verb* **accelerated, accelerating, accelerates.** To speed up: *The airplane began to accelerate as it neared the end of the runway.*

ad·a·mant /**ăd′** ə mənt/ -*adj.* Firm; not giving in easily: *Our teacher was adamant about the deadline for the assignment.*

ad·dic·tion /ə **dĭk′** shən/ -*noun* The condition of being unable to do without something, especially dependence on a harmful drug.

ad·ja·cent /ə **jā′** sənt/ -*adj.* Being next to each other; side by side: *Her house is adjacent to the city park.*

ad·journ /ə **jûrn′**/ -*verb* To stop for a time: *The court proceedings will adjourn for the weekend.*

ad·mit·tance /ăd **mĭt′** ns/ -*noun* Permission to enter: *In order to gain admittance to the concert, we needed a ticket.*

ad·ver·si·ty /ăd **vûr′** sĭ tē/ -*noun,* plural **adversities.** Hardship, misfortune, or great suffering: *Many people overcome adversity and lead successful lives.*

af·firm /ə **fûrm′**/ -*verb* To state firmly to be true; declare positively: *The mayor will affirm his belief that the midnight basketball league is good for the city.*

af·flu·ent /**ăf′** lōō ənt/ or /ə **flōō′** ənt/ -*adj.* Having much money or property; wealthy; rich: *The affluent couple takes expensive vacations every year.*

ag·gra·vate /**ăg′** rə vāt′/ -*verb* **aggravated, aggravating, aggravates. 1.** To make worse: *Instead of helping, interference may aggravate a situation.* **2.** To irritate: *Smudged glasses aggravate me.*

ag·i·tate /**ăj′** ĭ tāt′/ -*verb* **agitated, agitating, agitates.** To stir up; disturb; upset: *The candidate for mayor was careful not to agitate the crowd.*

al·le·vi·ate /ə **lē′** vē āt′/ -*verb* **alleviated, alleviating, alleviates.** To relieve; to make easier to bear; lessen: *During the flood many charities worked to alleviate the suffering of people whose houses were ruined by water.*

al·li·ance /ə **lī′** əns/ -*noun* An agreement in which nations, organizations, groups, or persons join together for a common cause or interest: *The alliance of the two hospitals was good for the community.*

al·ly /ə **lī′**/ or /**ăl′** ī/ -*noun,* plural **allies. 1.** Supporter: *The senator was an ally of the president.* **2.** A person, country, or group united for a common cause.

al·ter /ôl′ tər/ -*verb* To change; make different: *We had to alter our plans for the picnic because of the storm.*

am·big·u·ous /ăm bĭg′ yōō əs/ -*adj.* Having more than one meaning; unclear: *The ambiguous telephone message confused me, so I didn't return the call because I didn't know whom to call.*

an·a·lyze /ăn′ ə līz′/ -*verb* **analyzed, analyzing, analyzes.** To examine closely: *We should analyze our spending habits for the next three months.*

an·ti·bi·ot·ic /ăn′ tĭ bī ŏt′ ĭk/ -*noun* Medicine that is used in the prevention and treatment of diseases: *The doctor prescribed an antibiotic for my infection.*

an·ti·quat·ed /ăn′ tĭ kwā′ tĭd/ -*adj.* Out of date; too old to be useful: *We no longer use antiquated machines like typewriters in our office.*

an·ti·sep·tic /ăn′ tĭ sĕp′ tĭk/ -*adj.* Preventing infection by stopping the growth of germs: *The nurse applied an antiseptic lotion to the cut.*

anx·i·e·ty /ăng zī′ ĭ tē/ -*noun*, plural **anxieties.** A feeling of worry, uneasiness, or fear about what may happen: *Flying in an airplane causes anxiety in some people.*

ap·a·thy /ăp′ ə thē/ -*noun* A lack of interest, desire to act, or feeling: *The students' apathy is interfering with their learning.*

ap·pa·ra·tus /ăp′ ə rā′ təs/ or /ăp′ ə răt′ əs/ -*noun*, plural **apparatus** or **apparatuses.** A device or machine used for a particular purpose: *We bought an apparatus to wash the outside of the house.*

apt /ăpt/ -*adj.* Likely; having a tendency: *Without a map, a traveler is apt to get lost.*

ar·bi·trar·y /är′ bĭ trĕr′ ē/ -*adj.* Based on chance or opinion rather than a particular rule, law, or reason: *Vacations for the workers were scheduled in an arbitrary manner.*

as·cer·tain /ăs′ ər tān′/ -*verb* To find out: *The police said they would ascertain how the robbery was committed.*

as·sess /ə sĕs′/ -*verb* To make a judgment about; evaluate: *Teachers assess the work done by students.*

as·sure /ə shŏŏr′/ -*verb* **assured, assuring, assures. 1.** To state positively: *I assure you that I will not be late.* **2.** To guarantee.

at·test /ə tĕst′/ -*verb* To prove; show clearly: *His willingness to do whatever is needed attests to his positive attitude toward his job.*

a·vail /ə vāl′/ -*noun* Use, benefit, or advantage: *Julia's long hours of campaigning were to no avail; she lost the election for the local school board.*

a·vert /ə vûrt′/ -*verb* To avoid or keep from happening; prevent: *The driver of the car was able to avert an accident by sharply turning the steering wheel.*

bar·gain /bär′ gĭn/ -*noun* Something offered or bought at a low price: *Two pizzas for the price of one are a bargain.* -*verb* To discuss or argue over the terms of an agreement or price.

be·nev·o·lent /bə nĕv′ ə lənt/ -*adj.* Kind; generous: *The benevolent man took care of lost pets until the owners could be found.*

bla·tant /blāt′ nt/ -*adj.* Very obvious: *The child's blatant disobedience was noticed by everyone in the room.*

breach /brēch/ -*noun*, plural **breaches.** A violation; break: *The company lost many customers because of a breach of contract.* -*verb* To make a hole or gap in.

ca·pa·ble /kā′ pə bəl/ -*adj.* Having the ability; able: *Monarch butterflies are capable of migrating long distances.*

cap·i·tal /kăp′ ĭ tl/ -*noun* **1.** Money or wealth owned and used to make more money or wealth. **2.** The city where the seat of a government is located.

ca·su·al·ty /kăzh′ ōō əl tē/ -*noun*, plural **casualties.** A person who is injured or killed in an accident: *Tyrone became a casualty when a drunken driver ran into him.*

cha·ot·ic /kā ŏt′ ĭk/ -*adj.* In a state of great confusion or disorder: *The preparations for the party seemed chaotic, but actually they were well organized.*

char·ac·ter·is·tic /kăr′ ək tə rĭs′ tĭk/ -*noun* A typical feature or quality that sets something apart from others: *Loyalty to its owner is an important characteristic for a dog to have.*

chron·ic /krŏn′ ĭk/ -*adj.* Lasting a long time or coming back frequently: *His chronic cough never got better.*

chron·o·log·i·cal /krŏn′ ə lŏj′ ĭ kəl/ -*adj.* Arranged in the order in which events occur: *The family's birthdays were arranged in chronological order in the memory book.*

cir·cum·stance /sûr′ kəm stăns′/ -*noun* A condition, act, or event that is connected with and usually affects another event: *When planning the picnic, we had to consider a circumstance like bad weather.*

cir·cum·vent /sûr′ kəm vĕnt′/ -*verb* **1.** To get around by cleverness or trickery: *By choosing his words carefully, the candidate was able to circumvent the question.* **2.** To go around: *Because of the construction, we had to circumvent the intersection.*

cli·max /klī′ măks′/ -*noun* The point of greatest interest or excitement, usually happening near the end: *The climax of the movie was so exciting that we watched it again.*

co·her·ent /kō hîr′ ənt/ or /kō hĕr′ ənt/ -*adj.* Organized logically; easy to understand: *The student's answer was so coherent that the teacher applauded her.*

col·lab·o·ra·tion /kə lăb′ ə rā′ shən/ -*noun* Working together: *The collaboration of the scientists resulted in the discovery of a new medicine.*

com·pen·sate /kŏm′ pən sāt′/ -*verb* **compensated, compensating, compensates.** To pay or reimburse: *The store owner will compensate me for the work I did.*

com·pli·ca·tion /kŏm′ plĭ kā′ shən/ -*noun* Something that creates difficulty or adds more problems: *A lack of sleep may be a complication when one is ill.*

com·po·nent /kəm pō′ nənt/ -*noun* A necessary part of the whole: *A monitor is one component of a computer workstation.*

com·pre·hen·sive /kŏm′ prĭ hĕn′ sĭv/ -*adj.* Covering a broad range of material; thorough: *The examination for a real estate license is comprehensive.*

com·pul·so·ry /kəm pŭl′ sə rē/ -*adj.* Required: *In many states it is compulsory for a person riding in a car to fasten the seat belt.*

con·cept /kŏn′ sĕpt′/ -*noun* A general idea or understanding, especially based on one's observation, knowledge, or experience: *I had a concept of how to wallpaper a room after I watched a professional do it.*

con·cise /kən sīs′/ -*adj.* Expressing what is meant in a few words; short and clear: *The acceptance speech was concise.*

con·firm /kən **fûrm'**/ *-verb* To make certain; to prove to be true: *It is a good idea to confirm your hotel reservations before taking a trip.*

con·strue /kən **strōō'**/ *-verb* **construed, construing, construes.** To explain; interpret: *I could not construe the meaning behind the poem.*

con·tam·i·nate /kən **tăm'** ə nāt'/ *-verb* **contaminated, contaminating, contaminates.** To make dirty or impure by contact; pollute: *Dirty kitchen utensils may contaminate food.*

con·tra·dic·to·ry /kŏn' trə **dĭk'** tə rē/ *-adj.* Opposite to; not in agreement with: *The newspaper article was contradictory to the report on the television newscast.*

con·tro·ver·sy /**kŏn'** trə vûr' sē/ *-noun*, plural **controversies.** A disagreement, especially one that leads to much discussion: *The controversy concerning the use of wetlands will continue for many years.*

con·ven·tion·al /kən **věn'** shə nəl/ *-adj.* Following accepted practices; ordinary: *We celebrated the holiday in a conventional way.*

con·vey /kən **vā'**/ *-verb* **1.** To carry or transmit: *Computers make it possible to convey messages around the world very quickly.* **2.** To communicate: *Please convey our congratulations to the new parents.*

coun·sel /**koun'** səl/ *-verb* To advise: *The teacher counseled the students to get good grades.*

cur·tail /kər **tāl'**/ *-verb* To cut short; reduce; lessen: *Because of the severe snowstorm, after-school events were curtailed.*

de·fin·i·tive /dĭ **fĭn'** ĭ tĭv/ *-adj.* Complete; final; decisive: *The candidate won the election with a definitive margin of votes.*

de·grade /dĭ **grād'**/ *-verb* **degraded, degrading, degrades.** To lower in value, rank, or character: *A house that looks as if it has not been painted in many years may degrade the neighborhood.*

de·lib·er·ate /dĭ **lĭb'** ər ĭt/ *-adj.* Done on purpose; intentional: *The referee gave the team a penalty for committing a deliberate foul.* *-verb* /dĭ **lĭb'** ə rāt'/ To think or discuss carefully.

de·mor·al·ize /dĭ **môr'** ə lĭz'/ or /dĭ **mŏr'** ə lĭz'/ *-verb* **demoralized, demoralizing, demoralizes.** To lower the confidence of; discourage: *Losing a job may demoralize a person.*

dense /děns/ *-adj.* **-denser, densest.** Crowded or packed closely together: *It is easy to get lost in a dense forest.*

de·plete /dĭ **plēt'**/ *-verb* **depleted, depleting, depletes.** To reduce or decrease the amount; use up: *Running the marathon will deplete a person's energy.*

de·pres·sion /dĭ **prĕsh'** ən/ *-noun* A mental illness, characterized by continuing sadness, dejection, and despair, that may interfere with a person's ability to function normally.

de·prive /dĭ **prīv'**/ *-verb* **deprived, depriving, deprives. 1.** To take away something: *The judge said the law was unfair because it deprived people of their right to free speech.* **2.** To keep from having.

de·rog·a·to·ry /dĭ **rŏg'** ə tôr' ē/ *-adj.* Insulting; belittling: *Amy was very upset by the derogatory remarks that her friend made about her.*

de·spon·dent /dĭ **spŏn'** dənt/ *-adj.* Feeling depressed, dejected, or discouraged: *The woman was despondent after her mother died.*

de·tract /dĭ **trăkt**′/ –*verb* To reduce in value, quality, or importance: *A sloppy appearance might detract from what a person says.*

de·vi·ate /**dē**′ vē āt′/ –*verb* **deviated, deviating, deviates.** To move away from something; to turn aside from something: *If you deviate from the directions, you may get lost.*

de·vise /dĭ **vīz**′/ –*verb* **devised, devising, devises.** To plan; create; invent; prepare: *The leaders of the community devised a way to involve more people in charitable activities.*

de·void /dĭ **void**′/ –*adj.* Completely without; lacking: *The room was devoid of any bright colors.*

di·ag·nose /**dī**′ əg nōs′/ or /**dī**′ əg nōz′/ –*verb* **diagnosed, diagnosing, diagnoses.** To identify an illness by careful examination and study of symptoms: *Doctors are able to diagnose many more illnesses today than they could two hundred years ago.*

di·gress /dĭ **grĕs**′/ or /dī **grĕs**′/ To wander or depart from the main topic in speaking or writing: *When the speaker began to digress from the main topic, the audience became restless.*

dis·cern /dĭ **sûrn**′/ or /dĭ **zûrn**′/ –*verb* **1.** To be aware of or recognize with the eyes or intellect: *Sometimes a story may be so confusing that it is hard to discern the main theme.* **2.** To distinguish differences.

dis·cred·it /dĭs **krĕd**′ ĭt/ –*verb* **1.** To hurt the reputation of; disgrace: *A dishonest salesperson can discredit an entire company.* **2.** To destroy belief or trust in.

dis·crep·an·cy /dĭ **skrĕp**′ ən sē/ –*noun*, plural **discrepancies.** Difference; lack of agreement: *Nobody was able to explain the discrepancy between the written record and eyewitnesses' statements about what happened.*

dis·may /dĭs **mā**′/ –*verb* **1.** To fill with dread or fear: *The forecast of the hurricane dismayed the people living along the coast.* **2.** To discourage.

dis·miss /dĭs **mĭs**′/ –*verb* To reject as unimportant; put out of one's mind: *It is a mistake to dismiss instructions that come with new appliances.*

dis·pel /dĭ **spĕl**′/ –*verb* **dispelled, dispelling, dispels.** To drive away or make disappear; scatter: *The testimony at the trial dispelled many false rumors.*

dis·pense /dĭ **spĕns**′/ –*verb* **dispensed, dispensing, dispenses.** To give out; distribute: *The store dispenses coupons to its customers every Friday.*

dis·sen·sion /dĭ **sĕn**′ shən/ –*noun* A difference of opinion; disagreement: *The dissension among the team members caused them to lose the game.*

dis·tort /dĭ **stôrt**′/ –*verb* To twist or bend out of normal shape: *The mirror distorted the shape of the body.*

dis·trib·u·tor /dĭ **strĭb**′ yə tər/ –*noun* A person or company that sells things to buyers: *A distributor of exercise machines sent me a catalog.*

ec·o·nom·ics /ĕk′ ə **nŏm**′ ĭks/ or /ē′ kə **nŏm**′ ĭks/ –*noun* The science that deals with the study of money, goods, and services.

e·lec·tor·ate /ĭ **lĕk**′ tər ĭt/ –*noun* All of the people who have the right to vote in an election: *The electorate now includes any citizen who is eighteen years or older.*

el·i·gi·ble /**ĕl**′ ĭ jə bəl/ –*adj.* Qualified: *To be eligible for the job, a person must have experience doing that kind of work.*

e·lu·sive /ĭ lōō′ sĭv/ or /ĭ lōō′ zĭv/ -*adj*. Hard to describe, explain, or understand: *Understanding why a person likes certain music may be elusive.*

e·man·ci·pate /ĭ măn′ sə pāt′/ -*verb* **emancipated, emancipating, emancipates.** To free from slavery, control, or restraint.

em·broil /ĕm broil′/ -*verb* **1.** To throw into confusion: *An early snowstorm could embroil the whole city.* **2.** To involve in an argument or conflict.

e·mo·tion·al /ĭ mō′ shə nəl/ -*adj*. Relating to mental feelings, such as happiness, sadness, or anger: *The tired child was very emotional.*

em·u·late /ĕm′ yə lāt′/ -*verb* **emulated, emulating, emulates.** To try to equal or do better than, especially by copying or imitating: *Younger children often emulate their older brothers or sisters.*

en·deav·or /ĕn dĕv′ ər/ -*verb* To make a serious attempt; try: *The students always endeavor to pay attention to the teacher.* -*noun* A serious attempt.

en·dorse /ĕn dôrs′/ -*verb* **endorsed, endorsing, endorses.** To support: *The union members were asked to endorse the proposed contract.*

en·tice /ĕn tīs′/ -*verb* **enticed, enticing, entices.** To lead on by offering hope or desire; tempt: *The wonderful smell of the popcorn enticed me to buy some.*

ep·och /ĕp′ ək/ or /ē′ pŏk′/ -*noun* A period of time in history marked by certain events, characteristics, or developments: *The rise of the computer has marked the epoch of technology.*

er·rat·ic /ĭ răt′ ĭk/ -*adj*. Changeable; unpredictable: *The erratic movements of the dog indicated that it was lost.*

er·ro·ne·ous /ĭ rō′ nē əs/ -*adj*. Containing error; mistaken: *The erroneous directions were corrected before they were printed.*

eth·nic /ĕth′ nĭk/ -*adj*. Relating to a group of people who share a racial, religious, or cultural background: *The United States is made up of a variety of ethnic groups.*

ex·ceed /ĭk sēd′/ -*verb* **1.** To go beyond the limit of: *If you exceed the speed limit, you may get a ticket.* **2.** To be greater than: *She often exceeds my expectations.*

ex·em·pla·ry /ĭg zĕm′ plə rē/ -*adj*. Worthy of being an example for imitation; praiseworthy: *The teacher congratulated the children for their exemplary behavior during the field trip.*

ex·or·bi·tant /ĭg zôr′ bĭ tənt/ -*adj*. Going beyond reasonable limits; great or extreme; excessive: *I thought that the price of the new house was exorbitant.*

ex·pe·di·ent /ĭk spē′ dē ənt/ -*adj*. Suitable, useful, or appropriate for a certain situation: *It is expedient to organize your tools and materials before you begin a project.*

ex·pire /ĭk spīr′/ -*verb* **expired, expiring, expires.** To come to an end: *My driver's license will expire at the end of the year.*

ex·plic·it /ĭk splĭs′ ĭt/ -*adj*. Clearly defined, stated, or expressed: *George needed the money for the explicit reason of buying a new car.*

ex·tra·ne·ous /ĭk strā′ nē əs/ -*adj*. Not belonging; not essential: *Most of the explanation was extraneous to my question.*

fa·cil·i·tate /fə sĭl′ ĭ tāt′/ -*verb* **facilitated, facilitating, facilitates.** To make easier; aid: *Automobiles today have more equipment to facilitate driving than ever before.*

fea·si·ble /fē′ zə bəl/ -adj. Able to be done or carried out; possible: *We now know that travel in space is feasible.*

fla·grant /flā′ grənt/ -adj. Openly outrageous, bad, or wrong: *The employee was fired for flagrant violations of company rules.*

fluc·tu·ate /flŭk′ choo āt′/ -verb **fluctuated, fluctuating, fluctuates.** To change, vary, or waver: *The price of gasoline fluctuates throughout the year.*

for·feit /fôr′ fĭt/ -verb To lose or have to give up as a penalty for some crime, fault, or mistake: *The team had to forfeit the game because it didn't have enough players.*

for·mi·da·ble /fôr′ mĭ də bəl/ -adj. 1. Difficult to do or overcome: *Learning how to use a computer seemed like a formidable task.* 2. Causing fear or alarm.

for·mu·late /fôr′ myə lāt′/ -verb **formulated, formulating, formulates.** To plan or develop in a clear, careful, orderly way: *Before beginning a home repair project, you should formulate a plan for doing it.*

fos·ter /fô′ stər/ or /fŏs′ tər/ -verb To encourage the growth or development of: *The company tried to foster a spirit of cooperation among its employees.*

frail /frāl/ -adj. Physically weak: *The old man was mentally strong, but his body was frail.*

fran·chise /frăn′ chīz′/ -noun The right to vote. *Even though people have the franchise, some choose not to vote.*

fru·gal /froo′ gəl/ -adj. Careful not to waste money; thrifty: *The frugal man saved enough money to buy a vacation house on the Gulf of Mexico.*

fun·da·men·tal /fŭn′ də měn′ tl/ -adj. Basic; essential: *Beginning a sentence with a capital letter is a fundamental rule.*

ge·ner·ic /jə něr′ ĭk/ -adj. Not protected by a trademark, so not having a brand name: *The generic medicine was cheaper than the brand-name medicine.*

ha·bit·u·al /hə bĭch′ oo əl/ -adj. Frequent; done repeatedly: *The student's habitual tardiness resulted in a Saturday detention.*

har·ass /hăr′ əs/ or /hə răs′/ -verb To bother, irritate, disturb, or torment repeatedly: *People who work in customer service can lose their jobs if they harass customers.*

haz·ard /hăz′ ərd/ -noun A danger; risk: *Potholes in the road can be a hazard to drivers.*

her·i·tage /hěr′ ĭ tĭj/ -noun Something that is handed down from one generation to the next; a tradition: *He is proud of his Native-American heritage.*

ho·mo·ge·ne·ous /hō′ mə jē′ nē əs/ or /hō′ mə jēn′ yəs/ -adj. Made up of similar parts: *The neighborhood was not homogeneous; it had people from many backgrounds.*

hos·pi·ta·ble /hŏs′ pĭ tə bəl/ or /hŏ spĭt′ ə bəl/ -adj. Welcoming others in a friendly, generous, and open-minded manner: *The hospitable greeting made everyone feel at ease.*

hu·mane /hyoo mān′/ -adj. Kind; merciful; compassionate: *People should treat their pets in a humane manner.*

i·dyl·lic /ī dĭl′ ĭk/ -adj. Simple, easy, peaceful, and charming: *The artist painted an idyllic scene.*

im·pair /ĭm pâr′/ -verb To weaken or damage the strength, quality, or value of: *A heavy fog may impair your vision if you are driving a car.*

im·pede /ĭm pēd´/ -*verb* **impeded, impeding, impedes.** To slow down; delay; hinder: *An accident on the highway may impede traffic.*

im·per·a·tive /ĭm pĕr´ ə tĭv/ -*adj.* Absolutely required or necessary; unavoidable: *It is imperative that workers treat each other with respect.*

im·per·ti·nent /ĭm pûr´ tn ənt/ -*adj.* Boldly rude or insulting: *I regretted the impertinent remark as soon as I said it.*

im·plic·it /ĭm plĭs´ ĭt/ -*adj.* Meant or understood without being directly stated: *The viewers' enjoyment as they watched the film was implicit through their facial expressions.*

in·dis·pen·sa·ble /ĭn´ dĭ spĕn´ sə bəl/ -*adj.* Necessary; essential: *A life jacket is indispensable if one is in a boat on the ocean.*

in·dulge /ĭn dŭlj´/ -*verb* **indulged, indulging, indulges.** To allow oneself to take pleasure in or enjoy doing something: *I like to indulge in reading a good mystery book.*

in·er·tia /ĭ nûr´ shə/ -*noun* The tendency to resist change or action: *Although we knew that we had to finish the project, our inertia kept us from completing it.*

in·fe·ri·or /ĭn fîr´ ē ər/ -*adj.* Low or lower in quality, value, or importance: *The item was marked down because its inferior workmanship was obvious.*

in·flam·ma·tion /ĭn´ flə mā´ shən/ -*noun* Redness, swelling, pain, or heat caused by a reaction to injury, infection, or irritation.

in·flu·en·tial /ĭn floo ĕn´ shəl/ -*adj.* Having the ability or power to produce an effect or change in others: *The senator is an influential person in Congress.*

in·frac·tion /ĭn frăk´ shən/ -*noun* A breaking of a rule or law; violation: *She lost her driver's license because she had so many traffic infractions.*

in·her·ent /ĭn hîr´ ənt/ or /ĭn hĕr´ ənt/ -*adj.* Being a permanent or basic part of a thing or person: *Their inherent honesty has earned them great respect.*

in·i·tia·tive /ĭ nĭsh´ ə tĭv/ -*noun* The lead; the first step: *The woman took the initiative and started a campaign to clean up her neighborhood.*

in·oc·u·late /ĭ nŏk´ yə lāt´/ -*verb* **inoculated, inoculating, inoculates.** To inject a substance, such as a vaccine or serum, that protects a person or animal against disease: *Doctors inoculate babies to protect them against many diseases.*

in·sid·i·ous /ĭn sĭd´ ē əs/ -*adj.* Working in a secretly harmful manner: *The insidious disease was difficult to diagnose.*

in·sist /ĭn sĭst´/ -*verb* To demand firmly: *Companies insist that workers report to work on time.*

in·sti·tu·tion /ĭn´ stĭ too´ shən/ or /ĭn´ stĭ tyoo´ shən/ -*noun* An organization devoted to a particular purpose, especially one dedicated to public service: *The educational institution has helped many students.*

in·sur·gent /ĭn sûr´ jənt/ -*noun* A person who rebels against authority; a rebel: *The insurgent led a protest in front of the courthouse.*

in·te·gral /ĭn´ tĭ grəl/ or /ĭn tĕg´ rəl/ -*adj.* Necessary to make something complete; essential: *Wheels are an integral part of an automobile.*

in·tense /ĭn tĕns´/ -*adj.* **intenser, intensest.** Very strong; great in degree: *The intense storm damaged many homes.*

in·ter·fer·ence /ĭn′ tər **fĭr′** əns/ -*noun* The act of getting in the way of something: *The girl did not appreciate her friend's interference with her affairs.*

in·ter·vene /ĭn′ tər **vēn′**/ -*verb* **intervened, intervening, intervenes. 1.** To come between in order to change or prevent: *The police intervened in the argument between the men.* **2.** To come between certain events or time.

in·ti·mate /ĭn′ tə mĭt/ -*adj.* **1.** Familiar; closely associated: *The classmates have been intimate friends since first grade.* **2.** Personal; private.

in·val·u·able /ĭn **văl′** yo͞o ə bəl/ -*adj.* Priceless: *I learned many invaluable lessons from my parents.*

in·ves·tor /ĭn **vĕs′** tər/ -*noun* A person who buys part of a company or property for the purpose of obtaining profit or income.

in·volve /ĭn **vŏlv′**/ -*verb* **involved, involving, involves.** To include as a necessary part or condition; require: *Getting an education involves a great deal of hard work.*

jar·gon /**jär′** gən/ -*noun* The specialized language used in a certain job or profession: *The jargon used by people who work with computers is sometimes confusing.*

lax /lăks/ -*adj.* Careless; not strict: *The baby sitter was lax in enforcing the house rules.*

leg·is·la·tion /lĕj′ ĭ **slā′** shən/ -*noun* A law or group of laws made or passed: *Congress passed legislation that will make airports safer.*

le·ni·en·cy /**lē′** nē ən sē/ or /**lēn′** yən sē/ -*noun* Mercy; tolerance: *Everyone in the court was surprised by the leniency of the sentence the convicted robber received.*

lev·y /**lĕv′** ē/ -*verb* **levied, levying, levies.** To collect or charge: *The county levies a tax on personal property such as automobiles.*

lin·ger /**lĭng′** gər/ -*verb* To stay a while; to be slow in leaving: *We plan to linger on the beach until sundown.*

lu·cra·tive /**lo͞o′** krə tĭv/ -*adj.* Producing a lot of money; profitable: *The boy's grass-cutting business was very lucrative.*

lux·u·ri·ous /lŭg **zho͝or′** ē əs/ or /lŭk **sho͝or′** ē əs/ -*adj.* Characterized by giving pleasure or comfort but not being necessary: *The famous actress stayed at the luxurious hotel because she liked to be pampered.*

mal·a·dy /**măl′** ə dē/ -*noun*, plural **maladies.** A sickness, disease, or disorder of some sort: *Most of the students had the same malady, so the class was called off.*

mal·func·tion /măl **fŭngk′** shən/ -*verb* To fail to work properly: *If the furnace malfunctions, call a technician.* -*noun* A failure to work properly.

ma·neu·ver /mə **no͞o′** vər/ or /mə **nyo͞o′** vər/ -*verb* To move skillfully or carefully: *The ambulance had to maneuver through traffic to get to the accident.* -*noun* A skillful or planned move.

mas·quer·ade /măs′ kə **rād′**/ -*verb* **masqueraded, masquerading, masquerades.** To look or act like something else; disguise; pose: *At Halloween children masquerade in many different costumes.*

me·di·ate /**mē′** dē āt′/ -*verb* **mediated, mediating, mediates.** To work with two sides to settle differences or arguments: *Often a teacher will mediate when two students disagree with each other.*

men·tor /mĕn′ tôr′/ or /mĕn′ tər/ -noun A wise and trusted advisor: *A mentor can help an employee make career decisions.*

me·tic·u·lous /mĭ tĭk′ yə ləs/ -adj. Extremely careful: *Doctors must be meticulous when performing surgery.*

met·ro·pol·i·tan /mĕt′ rə pŏl′ ĭ tĕn/ -adj. Relating to or belonging to a large city: *The metropolitan newspaper covered news from all parts of the city.*

min·i·mum /mĭn′ ə məm/ -noun, plural **minimums** or **minima**. The least amount or degree possible: *I need a minimum of seven hours of sleep.*

mis·cel·la·ne·ous /mĭs′ ə lā′ nē əs/ -adj. Made up of a variety of different things: *We talked for hours about miscellaneous topics.*

mis·for·tune /mĭs fôr′ chən/ -noun Something bad that happens: *The chimney falling on top of the roof was a misfortune.*

mod·er·ate /mŏd′ ər ĭt/ -adj. Kept within reasonable limits: *Angela had a moderate amount of homework to do each evening.*

mo·tive /mō′ tĭv/ -noun Something that causes a person to act; reason: *Her motive for getting a second job was that she was saving to buy a house.*

mun·dane /mŭn dān′/ or /mŭn′ dān′/ -adj. Common; ordinary; practical: *Sometimes it is the mundane items rather than the expensive ones that add to a person's comfort.*

mus·ter /mŭs′ tər/ -verb To gather together or call up from within oneself: *I had to muster the courage to give the speech to 500 people.*

mu·tu·al /myōō′ chōō əl/ -adj. Shared; common: *Carol and Ann were good friends because of their mutual interest in sports.*

non·de·script /nŏn′ dĭ skrĭpt′/ -adj. Plain; without interesting features: *She wore a nondescript scarf.*

nov·ice /nŏv′ ĭs/ -noun A person who is new to something, such as an activity or job; beginner: *Even a novice can learn to use a computer.*

ob·jec·tive /əb jek′ tĭv/ -adj. Not influenced by personal feelings, opinions, or emotions: *Reporters are supposed to remain objective when writing a news story.*

o·bliv·i·ous /ə blĭv′ ē əs/ -adj. Not aware; unmindful: *He was concentrating so hard on reading his book that he was oblivious to everything else in the room.*

ob·scure /ŏb skyŏŏr′/ -adj. **obscurer, obscurest. 1.** Not well known: *The best-selling novel was written by an obscure author.* **2.** Hard to understand.

ob·struct /əb strŭkt′/ -verb To interfere with or get in the way of: *The protesters wanted to obstruct the new law even though the voters passed it.*

op·ti·mism /ŏp′ tə mĭz′ əm/ -noun A belief that everything will turn out for the best: *The enthusiastic speech filled the team with optimism.*

par·ti·san /pär′ tĭ zən/ -noun Relating to or characteristic of support for a particular party, cause, person, or idea: *Before an election, many partisan advertisements air on television.*

pe·des·tri·an /pə dĕs′ trē ən/ -noun A person traveling on foot: *The pedestrian waited for the green light before crossing the street.*

per·cep·tive /pər sĕp′ tĭv/ -adj. Having keen insight or understanding: *The perceptive clerk noticed that shoppers were not buying as many fattening foods.*

per·pe·trate /pûr′ pĭ trāt′/ *-verb* **perpetrated, perpetrating, perpetrates.** To commit or do something like a crime: *The police caught the persons who perpetrated the burglary.*

per·plex·ing /pər plĕks′ ĭng/ *-adj.* Confusing; puzzling: *The perplexing problem bothered me for weeks.*

per·se·vere /pûr′ sə vîr′/ *-verb* **persevered, persevering, perseveres.** To keep on following a course of action or purpose in spite of difficulty: *Even though the election seemed lost, the candidate said she would persevere until all votes were counted.*

per·sist·ence /pər sĭs′ təns/ *-noun* The act of continuing firmly and steadily in spite of difficulty: *Ryan's persistence paid off when he won the award for making the most improvement.*

per·ti·nent /pûr′ tn ənt/ *-adj.* Relating to the matter that is being considered: *All of the pertinent information was in the file folder.*

phar·ma·cy /fär′ mə sē/ *-noun* plural **pharmacies.** A place where medicines are sold; drugstore.

pic·tur·esque /pĭk′ chə rĕsk′/ *-adj.* Visually beautiful or charming, as in a picture: *We stopped the car to watch the picturesque sunset.*

plac·id /plăs′ ĭd/ *-adj.* Calm; peaceful; quiet: *The day we went fishing, the lake was placid.*

plau·si·ble /plô′ zə bəl/ *-adj.* Seemingly believable, true, or reasonable: *The teenager's excuse for being late was plausible.*

pon·der /pŏn′ dər/ *-verb* To think over carefully: *I had to ponder the problem for several days before I could offer a solution.*

por·tray /pôr trā′/ *-verb* **1.** To describe through the use of words: *The author portrayed the main character as sensitive to the feelings of others.* **2.** To show in a picture.

pose /pōz/ *-verb* **posed, posing, poses.** To present; to put forward: *The teacher posed a question that required much thought.*

pos·ter·i·ty /pŏ stĕr′ ĭ tē/ *-noun* Future generations of people: *She left a diary for posterity.*

post·pone /pōst pōn′/ *-verb* **postponed, postponing, postpones.** Put off until a later time: *We had to postpone the picnic because of the rain.*

pre·req·ui·site /prē rĕk′ wĭ zĭt/ *-adj.* Necessary; required beforehand: *A high school diploma is a prerequisite for that job.*

pre·scribe /prĭ skrīb′/ *-verb* **prescribed, prescribing, prescribes.** To set down as a rule or course of action to be followed. **-prescribed** *-adj.* Directed or ordered.

prev·a·lent /prĕv′ ə lənt/ *-adj.* Widespread; common: *The use of slang is prevalent in everyday conversation.*

pro·ba·tion /prō bā′ shən/ *-noun* A trial or test period to determine one's fitness for a job or membership: *The employee's probation lasted for six months.*

pro·cure /prō kyŏŏr′/ *-verb* **procured, procuring, procures.** To get or acquire: *Ron hoped to procure an unusual baseball card at the auction.*

pro·fi·cient /prə fĭsh′ ənt/ *-adj.* Able to do something well; skillful; expert: *The carpenter is proficient at building houses.*

pro·lif·er·ate /prə **lĭf'** ə rāt'/ –*verb* **proliferated, proliferating, proliferates.** To increase, spread, or grow rapidly: *The number of people using computers proliferates each year.*

pro·pose /prə **pōz'**/ –*verb* **proposed, proposing, proposes.** To suggest for consideration or acceptance: *The mayor proposed a new bus route that would benefit more people in the city.*

pros·per·ous /**prŏs'** pər əs/ –*adj.* Having a lot of money, profit, or success: *The little mountain village became prosperous when tourists started visiting it.*

pru·dent /**prood'** ənt/ –*adj.* Careful; sensible; wise: *A prudent shopper compares prices before making a purchase.*

quan·da·ry /**kwŏn'** də rē/ or /**kwŏn'** drē/ –*noun* A state of difficulty, uncertainty, or hesitation; predicament: *The girl was in a quandary about which college to attend.*

re·dress /rĭ **drĕs'**/ or /**rē'** drĕs/ –*noun* Something given or done to correct a wrong. –*verb* To set right; correct; remedy.

re·fer·ral /rĭ **fûr'** əl/ –*noun* The act or instance of directing or sending a person to someone else for help or information: *I asked for a referral to a mechanic who repaired antique cars.*

re·frain /rĭ **frān'**/ –*verb* To hold oneself back from doing something: *Please refrain from talking during the movie.*

re·ha·bil·i·ta·tion /rē' hə bĭl' ĭ **tā'** shən/ –*noun* The restoration of one's good name, status, or privileges: *The desire to succeed is a key part of any rehabilitation program.*

re·in·force /rē' ĭn **fôrs'**/ –*verb* **reinforced, reinforcing, reinforces.** To strengthen: *To reinforce the message in the telephone call, I also sent a letter.*

rel·e·vant /**rĕl'** ə vənt/ –*adj.* Related or having to do with the matter at hand: *The judge allowed only questions that were relevant to the case being tried.*

re·li·a·ble /rĭ **lī'** ə bəl/ –*adj.* Dependable; worthy of trust: *The reliable employee had never missed a day of work.*

re·mu·ner·a·tion /rĭ myōo' nə **rā'** shən/ –*noun* A payment for services, goods, or losses: *My remuneration for the job was satisfactory.*

re·plen·ish /rĭ **plĕn'** ĭsh/ –*verb* Refill or add a new supply: *When we returned home, we had to replenish the supplies we used for our camping trip.*

re·proach /rĭ **prōch'**/ –*noun,* plural **reproaches.** Blame; criticism: *The employee did not think he deserved the reproach from the supervisor.* –*verb* To blame; criticize.

re·scind /rĭ **sĭnd'**/ –*verb* To make not legally valid; cancel; repeal: *Congress rescinded the law requiring a fifty-five m.p.h. speed limit on the interstate highways.*

res·i·den·tial /rĕz' ĭ **dĕn'** shəl/ –*adj.* Having to do with where people live: *The streets in the residential parts of the city needed to be repaired.*

re·sil·ience /rĭ **zĭl'** yəns/ –*noun* The power or ability to recover quickly or easily: *Tom's resilience after his house was destroyed in the tornado was admirable.*

re·stric·tion /rĭ **strĭk'** shən/ –*noun* Something that establishes certain limits; limitation: *During the festival there will be a restriction on automobile traffic.*

re·tain /rĭ **tān′**/ -*verb* To keep in one's possession: *People retain copies of their tax forms for many years.*

re·ten·tion /rĭ **tĕn′** shən/ -*noun* The ability to remember or hold on to: *My retention of interesting information is better than it is of boring information.*

re·trieve /rĭ **trēv′**/ -*verb* **retrieved, retrieving, retrieves.** To get back; recover: *Nancy had to retrieve the ball from the neighbor's yard.*

ru·di·ment /**rōō′** də mənt/ -*noun,* Usually **rudiments.** The basic principle(s) of something: *To write well one must know the rudiments of grammar.*

ruse /rōōs/ or /rōōz/ -*noun* A trick: *Linda's ruse did not fool anyone.*

sa·vor /**sā′** vər/ -*noun* To enjoy with great delight: *Jamie likes to savor a cup of tea in the morning.*

scru·ti·nize /**skrōōt′** n īz′/ -*verb* **scrutinized, scrutinizing, scrutinizes.** To look at or examine closely: *A jeweler will scrutinize a diamond to determine its value.*

se·clud·ed /sĭ **klōō′** dĭd/ -*adj.* Shut off or distant from others: *The only way to reach the secluded cabin was by foot because there was no road.*

se·cure /sĭ **kyōōr′**/ -*verb* **secured, securing, secures. 1.** To make sure or guarantee: *The Bill of Rights secures our freedom.* **2.** To get.

seg·re·gate /**sĕg′** rĭ gāt′/ -*verb* **segregated, segregating, segregates. 1.** To separate from others. **2.** To separate because of race or social class from the rest of society.

seg·re·gat·ed /**sĕg′** rĭ gāt′ əd/ -*adj.* Separated from others: *Segregated schools are illegal in the United States.*

seize /sēz/ -*verb* **seized, seizing, seizes.** To take away or grab by force: *The rebels tried to seize control of the government.*

sen·si·ble /**sĕn′** sə bəl/ -*adj.* Having or showing good judgment; reasonable: *Eating nutritious food is a sensible thing to do.*

so·ci·e·ty /sə **sī′** ĭ tē/ -*noun,* plural **societies.** A group of people sharing common interests, tradition, culture, or purposes: *Because of faster methods of communication, society is more informed today than ever before.*

spa·tial /**spā′** shəl/ -*adj.* Having to do with space: *She has a good understanding of spatial relationships.*

spon·ta·ne·ous /spŏn **tā′** nē əs/ -*adj.* Coming from natural or automatic impulses or desires; not planned: *When the play ended, the theater was filled with spontaneous applause.*

sta·tis·tic /stə **tĭs′** tĭk/ -*noun* A numerical fact that is collected and used as information about a particular subject.

sta·tis·tics /stə **tĭs′** tĭks/ -*noun* (used with a plural verb) A collection or set of data expressed in numbers: *The sales statistics show that our company is doing very well.*

strive /strīv/ -*verb* **strove, striven** or **strived, striving, strives.** To try hard; to make a great effort: *Successful companies strive to please their customers.*

sub·ju·gate /**sŭb′** jə gāt′/ -*verb* **subjugated, subjugating, subjugates.** To conquer, subdue, or bring under one's control: *The dictator tried to subjugate the people in his country.*

sub·mit /səb **mĭt′**/ -*verb* **submitted, submitting, submits.** To hand in for the consideration or decision of another: *The teacher told the students to submit their projects at the end of the week.*

sub·se·quent /sŭb′ sĭ kwĕnt′/ –*adj.* Following or happening later or as a result: *I made subsequent visits to the doctor after my surgery.*

sun·dry /sŭn′ drē/ –*adj.* Various: *I have a special drawer for sundry letters, bills, and cards.*

su·per·fi·cial /soō′ pər fĭsh′ əl/ –*adj.* Being shallow or located near the surface: *Even though the cut was superficial, the doctor put a bandage on it.*

sur·mise /sər′ mīz′/ –*verb* **surmised, surmising, surmises.** To guess with little or no evidence: *I can only surmise what caused the accident.*

sur·name /sûr′ nām′/ –*noun* One's family name: *There are many identical surnames in the telephone directory.*

sur·ren·der /sə rĕn′ dər/ –*verb* To give up something to another: *The man had to surrender his driver's license because of his reckless driving habits.*

sus·tain /sə stān′/ –*verb* **1.** To keep alive or in effect: *Exercise is needed to sustain good health.* **2.** To supply with necessities. **3.** To support from below.

syn·op·sis /sĭ nŏp′ sĭs/ –*noun,* plural **synopses.** A brief summary or outline of a written work, play, movie, or similar work: *I read a synopsis of the novel before reading the entire book.*

tac·tic /tăk′ tĭk/ –*noun* A plan or means used to achieve a goal: *The child's tactic for getting what she wanted was to continually ask for it.*

te·di·ous /tē′ dē əs/ –*adj.* Tiring and boring because of length or dullness: *Some jobs must be done even if they are tedious.*

ter·mi·nate /tûr′ mə nāt′/ –*verb* **terminated, terminating, terminates.** To end: *We both have to agree in order to terminate our contract.*

ter·mi·nol·o·gy /tûr′ mə nŏl′ ə jē/ –*noun,* plural **terminologies.** The special words used in a particular trade, art, science, or other subject: *The terminology used when discussing computer systems may seem confusing at first.*

thwart /thwôrt/ –*verb* To prevent or block from doing or happening: *The people were able to thwart the efforts of those who wanted to build a highway through a historic park.*

trans·ac·tion /trăn săk′ shən/ or /trăn zăk′ shən/ –*noun* A business affair, action, or deal: *The transaction at the bank took just a few minutes.*

treach·er·ous /trĕch′ ər əs/ –*adj.* **1.** Disloyal; deceitful: *The treacherous act was discovered before any harm was done.* **2.** Dangerous: *The icy road was treacherous.*

treas·ur·y /trĕzh′ ə rē/ –*noun,* plural **treasuries.** A place that keeps money, especially public funds: *The treasury is constantly being checked to make sure that its records are accurate.*

trite /trīt/ –*adj.* **triter, tritest.** Not interesting because of overuse or repetition: *Robert became bored with the trite conversation.*

un·der·lie /ŭn′ dər lī′/ –*verb* **underlay, underlain, underlying, underlies.** To be the basis or hidden cause of: *People may not know what underlies their problems.*

un·der·mine /ŭn′ dər mīn′/ –*verb* **undermined, undermining, undermines.** To weaken or destroy: *The constant criticism began to undermine my confidence.*

un·sight·ly /ŭn **sīt′** lē/ *-adj.* **unsightlier, unsightliest.** Unpleasant to look at; ugly: *The garbage on the front lawn was unsightly.*

va·cate /**vā′** kāt′/ or /vā **kāt′**/ *-verb* **vacated, vacating, vacates.** To move out; leave empty: *The robins vacate their nests every year.*

vac·cine /văk **sēn′**/ or /**văk′** sēn′/ *-noun* A substance containing weakened or killed disease germs that produces immunity against the disease.

va·ri·e·ty /və **rī′** ĭ tē/ *-noun*, plural **varieties.** A group or collection of many different things: *My aunt collects a variety of old dishes.*

ver·bal /**vûr′** bəl/ *-adj.* **1.** Expressed in speech rather than writing: *The verbal directions were so complicated, I was afraid that I would forget them.* **2.** Relating to, or made up of, words.

ver·bose /vər **bōs′**/ *-adj.* Wordy: *The verbose magazine article was difficult to understand.*

ver·sion /**vûr′** zhən/ *-noun* A description or account given from one point of view: *His version of what happened was different from mine.*

vie /vī/ *-verb* **vied, vying, vies.** To compete: *The two teams vied for the championship.*

vig·i·lant /**vĭj′** ə lənt/ *-adj.* Watchful; alert: *Parents must be vigilant when their children are learning to walk.*

vi·o·la·tion /vī′ ə **lā′** shən/ *-noun* The breaking or disregarding of a rule or law: *She was given a ticket for a parking violation.*

vir·tu·al /**vûr′** cho͞o əl/ *-adj.* Existing in reality, though not in actual fact or name.

vi·su·al·ize /**vĭzh′** o͞o ə līz′/ *-verb* **visualized, visualizing, visualizes.** To form a mental picture of: *To relieve stress I like to visualize a beach and the ocean.*

vo·lu·mi·nous /və **lo͞o′** mə nəs/ *-adj.* Of great size; quite large: *I had to research a voluminous amount of material about dogs to write an informed essay about them.*

vol·un·tar·y /**vŏl′** ən tĕr′ ē/ *-adj.* Made, done, or performed by one's own choice or free will: *The children's contribution to the art museum was voluntary.*

Personal Word List

Write any words that need more study. You can write words you see in this book, at work, or at home.

_____   _____   _____

_____   _____   _____

_____   _____   _____

_____   _____   _____

_____   _____   _____

_____   _____   _____

_____   _____   _____

_____   _____   _____

_____   _____   _____

_____   _____   _____

_____   _____   _____

_____   _____   _____

_____   _____   _____

_____   _____   _____

_____   _____   _____

_____   _____   _____

Alphabetical Word List

Word	Lesson	Word	Lesson	Word	Lesson
abide	9	bargain	2	demoralize	13
abnormal	8	benevolent	13	dense	11
abstract	23	blatant	22	deplete	3
academic	21	breach	9	depression	5
accelerate	8	capable	13	deprive	16
adamant	12	capital	17	derogatory	10
addiction	7	casualty	1	despondent	5
adjacent	4	chaotic	18	detract	10
adjourn	19	characteristic	11	deviate	3
admittance	7	chronic	6	devise	24
adversity	18	chronological	23	devoid	13
affirm	19	circumstance	1	diagnose	8
affluent	14	circumvent	20	digress	23
aggravate	22	climax	23	discern	23
agitate	11	coherent	15	discredit	9
alleviate	13	collaboration	22	discrepancy	24
alliance	13	compensate	6	dismay	13
ally	19	complication	5	dismiss	11
alter	12	component	17	dispel	22
ambiguous	23	comprehensive	21	dispense	3
analyze	2	compulsory	4	dissension	9
antibiotic	6	concept	23	distort	7
antiquated	20	concise	6	distributor	6
antiseptic	5	confirm	10	economics	17
anxiety	3	construe	20	electorate	19
apathy	24	contaminate	5	eligible	13
apparatus	3	contradictory	16	elusive	14
apt	22	controversy	18	emancipate	18
arbitrary	11	conventional	14	embroil	19
ascertain	10	convey	10	emotional	5
assess	9	counsel	13	emulate	22
assure	2	curtail	8	endeavor	1
attest	10	definitive	10	endorse	19
avail	15	degrade	4	entice	2
avert	22	deliberate	11	epoch	18

Word	Lesson	Word	Lesson	Word	Lesson
erratic	1	impertinent	9	maneuver	1
erroneous	22	implicit	23	masquerade	5
ethnic	16	indispensable	8	mediate	4
exceed	7	indulge	14	mentor	22
exemplary	22	inertia	24	meticulous	12
exorbitant	17	inferior	20	metropolitan	15
expedient	3	inflammation	5	minimum	4
expire	8	influential	20	miscellaneous	8
explicit	2	infraction	12	misfortune	13
extraneous	15	inherent	12	moderate	7
facilitate	21	initiative	10	motive	13
feasible	10	inoculate	5	mundane	14
flagrant	12	insidious	24	muster	24
fluctuate	2	insist	2	mutual	4
forfeit	1	institution	21	nondescript	14
formidable	15	insurgent	18	novice	2
formulate	23	integral	23	objective	10
foster	9	intense	7	oblivious	4
frail	5	interference	16	obscure	20
franchise	19	intervene	8	obstruct	19
frugal	17	intimate	10	optimism	24
fundamental	3	invaluable	11	partisan	20
generic	6	investor	17	pedestrian	1
habitual	9	involve	7	perceptive	24
harass	9	jargon	6	perpetrate	16
hazard	12	lax	12	perplexing	24
heritage	16	legislation	4	persevere	6
homogeneous	16	leniency	20	persistence	7
hospitable	16	levy	17	pertinent	21
humane	9	linger	14	pharmacy	6
idyllic	18	lucrative	17	picturesque	14
impair	7	luxurious	14	placid	14
impede	8	malady	6	plausible	23
imperative	9	malfunction	12	ponder	21

Word	Lesson	Word	Lesson	Word	Lesson
portray	18	savor	14	vacate	4
pose	2	scrutinize	4	vaccine	5
posterity	18	secluded	14	variety	8
postpone	8	secure	16	verbal	10
prerequisite	15	segregated	20	verbose	1
prescribed	1	seize	18	version	18
prevalent	16	sensible	8	vie	19
probation	11	society	3	vigilant	12
procure	1	spatial	23	violation	4
proficient	11	spontaneous	22	virtual	24
proliferate	3	statistic	1	visualize	21
propose	19	strive	12	voluminous	21
prosperous	17	subjugate	18	voluntary	7
prudent	2	submit	6		
quandary	24	subsequent	13		
redress	11	sundry	15		
referral	7	superficial	5		
refrain	2	surmise	24		
rehabilitation	20	surname	15		
reinforce	12	surrender	2		
relevant	15	sustain	16		
reliable	11	synopsis	21		
remuneration	17	tactic	19		
replenish	17	tedious	15		
reproach	22	terminate	11		
rescind	20	terminology	21		
residential	15	thwart	3		
resilience	20	transaction	3		
restriction	1	treacherous	16		
retain	6	treasury	17		
retention	21	trite	15		
retrieve	3	underlie	7		
rudiments	21	undermine	9		
ruse	19	unsightly	4		

Answer Key

Pre-test

Page 10: 1. C, 2. A, 3. D, 4. C, 5. A, 6. B, 7. B, 8. D, 9. C, 10. A

Page 11: 11. A, 12. C, 13. B, 14. B, 15. A, 16. C, 17. B, 18. C, 19. D, 20. A, 21. B, 22. D, 23. A, 24. B, 25. D, 26. A, 27. D, 28. C, 29. A, 30. B

Unit 1, Lesson 1

Page 13: 1. A, 2. B, 3. D, 4. D, 5. B, 6. C, 7. A, 8. D, 9. B, 10. C, 11. A, 12. D

Page 14: 1. restriction, 2. procure, 3. statistic, erratic; 4. prescribed, 5. circumstance, 6. forfeit, 7. casualty, 8. maneuver, 9. verbose, 10. endeavor, 11–12. casualty, pedestrian; 13. tis, statistic; 14. pro, procure; 15. pre, prescribed; 16. ver, maneuver; 17. rat, erratic; 18. feit, forfeit; 19. stance, circumstance; 20. tion, restriction

Page 15: 1. Unless . . . ., 2. Did . . . ?, 3. What . . . !, 4. The. . . ., 5–8. Answers will vary.

Page 16: pedestrian, Any, restriction, . . . casualty?

Lesson 2

Page 17: 1. D, 2. A, 3. D, 4. B, 5. C, 6. C

Page 18: 7. B, 8. D, 9. A, 10. D, 11. C, 12. B

Page 19: 1. bargain, 2. surrender, 3. pose, 4. analyze, 5. entice, novice; 6. fluctuate, 7. assure, 8. insist, 9. insist, 10. explicit, 11. entice, 12. prudent, 13. novice, 14. fluctuate, 15. refrain, 16. analyze

Page 20: 1. insist, 2. radio, 3. finger, 4. court, 5. knife, 6. center, 7. install, 8. superior, 9. treasure, 10. flexible, 11. heroic, 12. lightning, 13. positive, 14. compact, 15. lamb

Page 21: insist, analyze, fluctuate, prudent

Lesson 3

Page 23: 1. C, 2. A, 3. B, 4. A, 5. D, 6. B, 7. C, 8. D, 9. C, 10. B, 11. A, 12. B

Page 24: 1. society, anxiety; 2. thwart, 3. apparatus, 4. transaction, 5. deplete, 6. society, retrieve, anxiety, expedient; 7. fundamental, 8. dispense, 9. proliferate, 10. deviate, 11. a, u, apparatus; 12. e, a, proliferate; 13. e, s, dispense; 14. w, a, thwart; 15. deplete, deviate; 16. thwart, transaction; 17. expedient, fundamental; 18. retrieve, society

Page 25: 1. . . . anxieties . . ., 2. . . . depleted . . ., 3. . . . friendliness . . ., 4. . . . imaginable . . ., 5. . . . arranging . . ., 6. . . . arrangement . . ., 7. . . . valuable . . ., 8. . . . steadily . . .

Page 26: retrieve, fundamental, apparatus, proliferate

Lesson 4

Page 27: 1. D, 2. A, 3. B, 4. B, 5. D, 6. C

Page 28: 7. B, 8. D, 9. A, 10. B, 11. C, 12. A

Page 29: 1. com·pul·so·ry, 2. leg·is·la·tion, 3. o·bliv·i·ous, 4. un·sight·ly, 5. legislation, 6. vacate, mediate; 7. degrade, 8. adjacent, vacate; 9. violation, 10. minimum, 11. adjacent, 12. unsightly, 13. scrutinize, 14. mutual, 15. scrutinize, 16. mediate, 17. adjecent, adjacent; 18. compulsury, compulsory; 19. oblivius, oblivious; 20. violasion, violation

Page 30: 1. . . . violation . . ., 2. . . . legislation . . ., 3. . . . invitation . . ., 4. . . . admiration . . ., 5. . . . combination . . .

Page 31: scrutinized, adjacent, mutual, minimum

Unit 1 Review

Page 32: 1. C, 2. D, 3. A, 4. B, 5. A, 6. C, 7. D, 8. A, 9. B, 10. D

Page 33: 11. B, 12. A, 13. C, 14. D, 15. C, 16. C, 17. B, 18. A, 19. C, 20. D

Unit 2, Lesson 5

Page 35: 1. C, **2.** B, **3.** D, **4.** C, **5.** A, **6.** B, **7.** D, **8.** A, **9.** D, **10.** C, **11.** B, **12.** A

Page 36: 1. complication, inflammation; **2.** superficial, **3.** contaminate, inoculate; **4.** depression, vaccine, inflammation; **5.** emotional, **6.** masquerade, **7.** frail, **8.** despondent, **9.** antiseptic, **10.** depression, **11.** quer, masquerade; **12.** des, despondent; **13.** oc, inoculate; **14.** i, contaminate; **15.** fi, superficial; **16.** (innoculate), inoculate, **17.** (frayl), frail, **18.** (anteseptic), antiseptic

Page 37: 1. antisocial, **2.** superimpose, **3.** supervise, **4.** antimagnetic, **5.** antidepressant, **6.** supersensitive

Page 38: vaccine, superficial, inflammation, despondent

Lesson 6

Page 39: 1. C, **2.** A, **3.** A, **4.** C, **5.** D, **6.** C

Page 40: 7. C, **8.** D, **9.** C, **10.** A, **11.** B, **12.** C

Page 41: 1. antibiotic, generic, chronic; **2.** jargon, submit; **3.** malady, pharmacy; **4.** persevere, **5.** pharmacy, **6.** antibiotic, **7.** compensate, **8.** retain, **9.** malady, **10.** retain, **11–16.** chronic, compensate, concise, distributor, generic, jargon; **17.** (concice), concise; **18.** (perseveer), persevere

Page 42: 1. . . . California . . .Grand Canyon., **2.** . . . Coast Guard Auxiliary . . ., **3.** . . . Tulip Avenue., **4.** . . . Stalinism., **5.** . . . Harvard . . ., **6.** . . . Protestantism . . ., **7.** Valumart Hardware., **8.** . . . Enrique . . . Puerto Rico . . . Americanized . . .

Page 43: retains, submit, pharmacy, compensate

Lesson 7

Page 45: 1. C, **2.** A, **3.** D, **4.** B, **5.** B, **6.** C, **7.** A, **8.** D, **9.** D, **10.** B, **11.** D, **12.** B

Page 46: 1. impair, **2.** addiction, admittance, referral; **3.** voluntary, **4.** admittance, **5.** exceed, **6.** intense, involve; **7.** voluntary, **8.** involve, **9.** exceed, **10.** moderate, **11.** referral, **12.** distort, **13.** underlie, **14.** d, t, addiction; **15.** i, e, underlie; **16.** e, c, persistence

Page 47: 1. spoiling, **2.** propeller, **3.** sealed, **4.** omitted, **5.** beginning, **6.** regrettable, **7.** occurrence, **8.** conferring, **9.** preferred, **10.** gossiping, **11.** forbidden, **12.** developed, **13.** repellent, **14.** bragging, **15.** patrolled, **16.** deposited

Page 48: addiction, moderate, exceed, persistence

Lesson 8

Page 49: 1. A, **2.** C, **3.** B, **4.** D, **5.** A, **6.** D

Page 50: 7. B, **8.** D, **9.** C, **10.** A, **11.** B, **12.** C

Page 51: 1–4. cur·tail, im·pede, ex·pire, post·pone; **5–8.** sen·si·ble, ab·nor·mal, in·ter·vene, di·ag·nose; **9.** miscellaneous, **10.** indispensable, sensible; **11.** accelerate, **12.** miscellaneous, **13.** postpone, **14.** variety, **15.** impede, **16.** diagnose, **17.** cel, accelerate; **18.** cur, curtail; **19.** sa, indispensable; **20.** vene, intervene

Page 52: 1. impersonal, **2.** imperfect, **3.** exclude, **4.** insubordinate, **5.** impolite, **6.** exhaust, **7.** expel, **8.** impatient, **9.** immune, **10.** extinct

Page 53: sensible, curtail, diagnose, miscellaneous

Unit 2 Review

Page 54: 1. C, **2.** B, **3.** D, **4.** A, **5.** B, **6.** C, **7.** D, **8.** B, **9.** B, **10.** A, **11.** B, **12.** B

Page 55: 13. C, **14.** C, **15.** A, **16.** D, **17.** B, **18.** A, **19.** A, **20.** D, **21.** B, **22.** C, **23.** D, **24.** D

Unit 3, Lesson 9

Page 57: 1. C, 2. D, 3. A, 4. C, 5. B, 6. C, 7. D, 8. B, 9. D, 10. B, 11. C, 12. B

Page 58: 1. assess, harass; 2. humane, 3. impertinent, imperative; 4. discredit, 5. habitual, 6. breach, 7. dissension, 8. undermine, 9. abide, 10. foster, 11. harass, 12. assess, 13. discredit, 14. der, undermine; 15. tive, imperative; 16. ass, harass

Page 59: 1. . . . discount . . ., 2. . . . disclose . . ., 3. . . . disloyal . . ., 4. . . . disrupt . . ., 5. . . . disrepair . . ., 6. . . . distract . . .

Page 60: Assess, foster, impertinent, dissension

Lesson 10

Page 61: 1. D, 2. B, 3. A, 4. B, 5. A, 6. C

Page 62: 7. A, 8. B, 9. B, 10. B, 11. D, 12. A

Page 63: 1. objective, 2. convey, 3. ascertain, 4. attest, 5. verbal, 6. initiative, 7. detract, 8. confirm, 9. feasible, 10. derogatory, 11. initiative, 12. definitive, 13. feasible, 14. verbal, 15. objective, 16. detract, 17. attest, 18. derogatory, 19. ascertain, 20. convey

Page 64: 1. . . . residential . . ., 2. . . . traceable . . ., 3. . . . believable . . ., 4. . . . valuable . . ., 5. . . . prosperous . . ., 6. . . . seasonal . . .

Page 65: ascertain, feasible, definitive, Convey

Lesson 11

Page 67: 1. D, 2. C, 3. C, 4. A, 5. B, 6. B, 7. D, 8. A, 9. B, 10. B, 11. D, 12. D

Page 68: 1. dismiss, redress; 2. dense, 3. agitate, terminate, deliberate; 4. reliable, redress;

5. probation, proficient; 6. reliable, 7. arbitrary, 8. invaluable, reliable; 9. agitate, 10. proficient, 11. deliberate, characteristic, invaluable; 12. agitate, 13. probation, 14. reliable, 15. dismiss, 16. arbitrary

Page 69: 2. . . . noisier . . ., 3. . . . most expensive . . ., 4. . . . more ambitious . . ., 5. . . . merrier . . ., 6. . . . earliest . . .

Page 70: invaluable, reliable, proficient, redress

Lesson 12

Page 71: 1. C, 2. A, 3. C, 4. A, 5. C, 6. D

Page 72: 7. B, 8. C, 9. D, 10. B, 11. D, 12. C

Page 73: 1. strive, 2. reinforce, 3. lax, strive; 4. hazard, flagrant; 5. infraction, inherent; 6. meticulous, 7. lax, 8. alter, 9. infraction, malfunction; 10. adamant, 11–16. infraction, vigilant, adamant, inherent, reinforce, malfunction

Page 74: Answers will vary. Possible answers: 1. someone who gives money or help, 2. a disease or complaint, 3. threatening, deadly; 4. kind and gentle, 5. extremely harmful, 6. a condition caused by a lack of nourishment, 7. careless or bad treatment by a doctor or similar professional person, 8. a person who gets the funds or other benefits of another

Page 75: malfunction, alter, adamant, flagrant

Unit 3 Review

Page 76: 1. C, 2. A, 3. D, 4. A, 5. A, 6. C, 7. C, 8. A, 9. D, 10. B, 11. C, 12. D

Page 77: 13. C, 14. B, 15. A, 16. A, 17. B, 18. A, 19. A, 20. C, 21. B, 22. D, 23. C, 24. B

Unit 4, Lesson 13

Page 79: 1. A, **2.** B, **3.** A, **4.** D, **5.** A, **6.** D, **7.** C, **8.** B, **9.** D, **10.** A, **11.** D, **12.** B

Page 80: 1. capable, eligible; **2.** subsequent, benevolent; **3.** alleviate, alliance; **4.** devoid, demoralize; **5.** dismay, **6.** misfortune, **7.** counsel, **8.** se, subsequent; **9.** gi, eligible; **10.** nev, benevolent, **11.** void, devoid; **12.** vi, alleviate, **13.** (motiv), motive; **14.** (demorelize), demoralize; **15.** (dissmay), dismay; **16.** (misforchune), misfortune

Page 81: 1. . . . council . . ., **2.** . . . complement . . ., **3.** . . . alter . . ., **4.** . . . complimented . . ., **5.** . . . counseled . . ., **6.** . . . altar . . .

Page 82: subsequent, counseled, eligible, demoralized

Lesson 14

Page 83: 1. D, **2.** B, **3.** A, **4.** D, **5.** C, **6.** D

Page 84: 7. B, **8.** D, **9.** C, **10.** B, **11.** B, **12.** D

Page 85: 1. luxurious, **2.** savor, **3.** nondescript, **4.** affluent, **5.** secluded, **6.** conventional, **7.** linger, **8.** indulge, **9.** mundane, **10.** placid, **11.** indulge, **12.** linger, **13.** savor, **14.** e, p, nondescript; **15.** u, o, luxurious; **16.** t, a, conventional; **17.** q, u, picturesque; **18.** f, u, affluent

Page 86: 1. Hilda Simons, **2.** Jason Marcus, **3.** Manager, **4.** Ocean View Cabins, **5.** Massachusetts, **6.** comma, **7.** colon, **8.** comma, **9.** no, **10.** heading, **11.** yes, **12.** Fort Wayne, Indiana

Page 87: picturesque, savor, mundane, luxurious

Lesson 15

Page 89: 1. A, **2.** C, **3.** C, **4.** B, **5.** C, **6.** A, **7.** D, **8.** D, **9.** B, **10.** B, **11.** C, **12.** A

Page 90: 1. trite, **2.** sundry, **3.** surname, avail; **4.** residential, **5.** extraneous, tedious; **6.** surname, **7.** metropolitan, **8.** relevant, **9.** formidable, **10.** formidable, residential, prerequisite; **11.** co·her·ent, **12.** di·ver·sion, **13.** rel·e·vant, **14.** te·di·ous, **15.** trite, **16.** surname, **17.** coherent, **18.** extraneous

Page 91: 1. . . . prosperous . . ., **2.** . . . studious . . ., **3.** . . . marketable . . ., **4.** . . . ceremonial . . ., **5.** . . . acceptable . . ., **6.** . . . reliable . . .

Page 92: formidable, metropolitan, tedious, relevant

Lesson 16

Page 93: 1. B, **2.** B, **3.** A, **4.** D, **5.** C, **6.** C

Page 94: 7. C, **8.** D, **9.** B, **10.** D, **11.** C, **12.** A

Page 95: 1. treacherous, **2.** contradictory, **3.** prevalent, **4.** interference, **5.** hospitable, **6.** homogeneous, **7.** prevalent, **8.** ethnic, **9.** sustain, **10.** heritage, **11.** perpetrate, **12.** homogeneous, treacherous; **13–16.** de·prive, se·cure, sus·tain, eth·nic; **17.** prive, deprive; **18.** eth, ethnic; **19.** tage, heritage; **20.** ta, hospitable

Page 96: Answers may vary. Possible answers: **1.** within a vein, **2.** to come between or stop, **3.** between cities, **4.** within the school, **5.** between religious faiths, **6.** between continents, **7.** between libraries, **8.** within the galaxy, **9.** between religious denominations, **10.** a period between events

Page 97: Heritage, ethnic, prevalent, sustain

Unit 4 Review

Page 98: 1. B, **2.** C, **3.** A, **4.** B, **5.** D, **6.** A, **7.** C, **8.** B, **9.** A, **10.** D, **11.** B, **12.** C

Page 99: 13. B, **14.** A, **15.** C, **16.** D, **17.** D, **18.** B, **19.** C, **20.** B, **21.** A, **22.** A, **23.** C, **24.** A

Unit 5, Lesson 17

Page 101: 1. C, **2.** D, **3.** A, **4.** B, **5.** C, **6.** B, **7.** C, **8.** B, **9.** D, **10.** A, **11.** D, **12.** A

Page 102: 1. remuneration, replenish; **2.** treasury, **3.** prosperous, **4.** levy, **5.** capital, frugal; **6.** exorbitant, **7.** investor, **8.** economics, **9.** component, **10.** lucrative, **11.** ish, replenish; **12.** in, investor; **13.** treas, treasury; **14.** lu, lucrative; **15.** tant, exorbitant; **16.** fru, frugal; **17.** ~~componant~~, component; **18.** ~~levey~~, levy; **19.** ~~remunuration~~, remuneration; **20.** ~~prosperus~~, prosperous

Page 103: 1. my parents' tax return, **2.** teacher's answer, **3.** workers' demands, **4.** Norma's mailbox, **5.** Women's hats, **6.** her boss's office, **7.** the lions' loud roars, **8.** the river's edge

Page 104: investor, remuneration, replenish, prosperous

Lesson 18

Page 105: 1. D, **2.** A, **3.** C, **4.** C, **5.** A, **6.** D

Page 106: 7. B, **8.** D, **9.** D, **10.** A, **11.** B, **12.** A

Page 107: 1. seize, **2.** idyllic, **3.** adversity, **4.** chaotic, idyllic; **5.** epoch, **6.** version, **7.** insurgent, **8.** emancipate, **9.** controversy, **10.** subjugate, **11.** portray, **12.** seize, **13.** e, i, posterity; **14.** u, e, insurgent; **15.** o, i, chaotic; **16.** e, s, adversity; **17.** e, h, epoch; **18.** s, i, version; **19.** o, y, portray; **20.** c, i, emancipate

Page 108: 1. accurate, **2.** assemble, **3.** affection, **4.** accord, **5.** approve, **6.** asset, **7.** account, **8.** afflict, **9.** appoint, **10.** aggressive, **11.** allegation, **12.** accent, **13.** assignment, **14.** associate, **15.** affix

Page 109: emancipate, chaotic, epoch, subjugate

Lesson 19

Page 111: 1. C, **2.** D, **3.** B, **4.** B, **5.** A, **6.** B, **7.** A, **8.** C, **9.** B, **10.** D, **11.** C, **12.** A

Page 112: 1. ally, affirm; **2.** adjourn, affirm; **3.** electorate, **4.** embroil, **5.** ally, **6.** franchise, propose; **7.** propose, tactic; **8.** ruse, vie; **9.** obstruct, **10.** endorse, **11.** adjourn, **12.** broil, embroil; **13.** o, electorate; **14.** struct, obstruct

Page 113: 1. . . . race, religion, or sex., **2.** . . . women, African Americans, and the poor . . ., **3.** . . . in businesses, on farms, and in schools . . ., **4.** no commas needed, **5.** . . . stepped into the booth, closed the curtain, and cast his vote., **6.** no commas needed, **7.** . . . frowning, biting her·lip, and wringing her hands . . ., **8.** . . . register early, study the issues, and vote your beliefs.

Page 114: affirm, obstruct, . . . lies, misinformation, and similar tactics., adjourn

Lesson 20

Page 115: 1. D, **2.** A, **3.** B, **4.** C, **5.** D, **6.** A

Page 116: 7. B, **8.** C, **9.** D, **10.** C, **11.** A, **12.** B

Page 117: 1. leniency, **2.** resilience, **3.** rehabilitation, **4.** influential, **5.** circumvent, **6.** leniency, resilience; **7.** influential, inferior; **8.** obscure, **9.** rescind, **10.** construe, **11.** antiquated, **12.** partisan, circumvent; **13.** strue, construe; **14.** re, segregated; **15.** ti, antiquated; **16.** scure, obscure; **17.** or, inferior; **18.** bil, rehabilitation

Page 118: Answers may vary. Possible answers: **1.** the boundary line around an area, **2.** the moving of a substance like blood from one place or person to another, **3.** to change the place or order of two things, **4.** talking in a roundabout or indirect way, **5.** the act of circling or going around something, **6.** passing or moving by, **7.** the situation that surrounds a person or thing, **8.** to change the look or nature of something

Page 119: partisan, construe, inferior, rescind

Unit 5 Review

Page 120: 1. C, **2.** A, **3.** B, **4.** D, **5.** B, **6.** C, **7.** A, **8.** D, **9.** C, **10.** D, **11.** A, **12.** C

Page 121: 13. C, **14.** A, **15.** D, **16.** B, **17.** B, **18.** D, **19.** A, **20.** C, **21.** D, **22.** C, **23.** A, **24.** B

Unit 6, Lesson 21

Page 123: 1. D, 2. B, 3. A, 4. D, 5. B, 6. D, 7. C, 8. D, 9. B, 10. A, 11. A, 12. C

Page 124: 1. institution, retention; 2. ponder, 3. facilitate, 4. synopsis, 5. rudiments, 6. terminology, 7. comprehension, 8. pertinent, 9. voluminous, 10. visualize, 11. academic, 12. institution, 13. retention, 14. e, i, comprehensive; 15. s, z, visualize; 16. i, o, voluminous; 17. e, r, ponder; 18. y, i, synopsis

Page 125: 1. zoology, 2. criminology, 3. mineralogy, 4. mythology, 5. sociology, 6. psychology, 7. theology, 8. ecology, 9. bacteriology, 10. physiology, 11. technology, 12. geology

Page 126: rudiments, academic, voluminous, pertinent

Lesson 22

Page 127: 1. C, 2. A, 3. D, 4. A, 5. B, 6. D

Page 128: 7. B, 8. A, 9. D, 10. A, 11. B, 12. C

Page 129: 1. emulate, aggravate; 2. collaboration, 3. apt, 4. collaboration, aggravate, erroneous; 5. mentor, 6. exemplary, 7. reproach, 8. spontaneous, erroneous; 9. avert, 10. blatant, 11. apt, 12. a·vert, 13. bla·tant, 14. dis·pel, 15. ta, ous, spontaneous; 16. col, ra, collaboration; 17. u, late, emulate; 18. em, ry, exemplary; 19. tor, mentor; 20. proach, reproach

Page 130: Answers will vary. Possible answers: 1. cheap and showy in appearance, 2. refuse to do business or have anything to do with someone, 3. a place of great confusion and disorder, 4. a tight-fitting garment often worn by dancers, 5. whiskers grown down the side of a man's face in front of the ears, 6. to fascinate or hold spellbound

Page 131: dispel, collaboration, avert, emulate

Lesson 23

Page 133: 1. C, 2. B, 3. A, 4. D, 5. A, 6. C, 7. D, 8. B, 9. D, 10. A, 11. C, 12. B

Page 134: 1. concept, 2. digress, 3. concept, 4. implicit,

5. climax, 6. plausible, 7. chronological, 8. spatial, 9. ambiguous, 10. discern, 11. spatial, chronological, integral; 12. digress, 13. implicit, 14. abstract, 15. intagral, integral; 16. ambigous, ambiguous; 17. plausable, plausible; 18. digres, digress

Page 135: Answers may vary. Possible answers: 1. lasting for a long time or occurring time after time, 2. the speed or timing of the beats in music, 3. out of its time, old-fashioned; 4. living at the same time, 5. to occur at the same time, 6. a record of events as they occur during a period of time

Page 136: plausible, discern, implicit, integral

Lesson 24

Page 137: 1. A, 2. D, 3. D, 4. B, 5. C, 6. A

Page 138: 7. A, 8. D, 9. C, 10. B, 11. A, 12. D

Page 139: 1. perceptive, 2. insidious, inertia; 3. quandary, discrepancy, apathy; 4. virtual, 5. surmise, devise; 6. muster, 7. perplexing, 8. optimism, 9. insidious, 10. inertia, 11. i, i, optimism; 12. e, a, discrepancy; 13. e, i, perplexing; 14. u, e, muster; 15. i, a, virtual; 16. e, i, devise

Page 140: Answers will vary. Possible answers: 1. without morals, 2. shared feelings, 3. without government or law, 4. causing feelings of sorrow or pity, 5. not typical, 6. strong feeling of opposition

Page 141: devise, quandary, perplexing, insidious

Unit 6 Review

Page 142: 1. C, 2. B, 3. C, 4. A, 5. D, 6. B, 7. B, 8. D, 9. C, 10. A, 11. C, 12. B

Page 143: 13. C, 14. A, 15. D, 16. D, 17. A, 18. C, 19. B, 20. C, 21. A, 22. A, 23. D, 24. A

Post-test

Page 144: 1. B, 2. C, 3. A, 4. D, 5. C, 6. B, 7. A, 8. D, 9. C, 10. B

Page 145: 11. A, 12. D, 13. C, 14. B, 15. A, 16. C, 17. D, 18. A, 19. B, 20. B, 21. A, 22. D, 23. B, 24. D, 25. B, 26. A, 27. C, 28. A, 29. B, 30. C

Scoring Chart

Use this chart to find your score. Line up the number of items with the number correct. For example, if 14 out of 15 items are correct, the score is 93.3 percent.

Number Correct

Number of Items	5	6	7	8	9	10	11	12	13	14	15	16	17	18	19	20	21	22	23	24	25	26	27	28	29	30
5	100																									
6	83.3	100																								
7	71.4	85.7	100																							
8	62.5	75	87.5	100																						
9	55.5	66.7	77.7	88.9	100																					
10	50	60	70	80	90	100																				
11	45.4	54.5	63.6	72.7	81.8	90.9	100																			
12	41.7	50	58.3	66.7	75	83.3	91.7	100																		
13	38.5	46.1	53.8	61.5	69.2	76.9	84.6	92.3	100																	
14	35.7	42.8	50	57.1	64.3	71.4	78.5	85.7	92.8	100																
15	33.3	40	46.6	53.3	60	66.7	73.3	80	86.7	93.3	100															
16	31.2	37.5	43.7	50	56.2	62.5	68.7	75	81.2	87.5	93.7	100														
17	29.4	35.3	41.2	47	52.9	58.8	64.7	70.6	76.5	82.3	88.2	94.1	100													
18	27.8	33.3	38.9	44.4	50	55.5	61.1	66.7	72.2	77.8	83.3	88.9	94.4	100												
19	26.3	31.6	36.8	42.1	47.4	52.6	57.9	63.1	68.4	73.7	78.9	84.2	89.4	94.7	100											
20	25	30	35	40	45	50	55	60	65	70	75	80	85	90	95	100										
21	23.8	28.6	33.3	38.1	42.8	47.6	52.3	57.1	61.9	66.7	71.4	76.1	80.9	85.7	90.5	95.2	100									
22	22.7	27.3	31.8	36.4	40.9	45.4	50	54.5	59.1	63.6	68.1	72.7	77.2	81.8	86.4	90.9	95.4	100								
23	21.7	26.1	30.4	34.8	39.1	43.5	47.8	52.1	56.5	60.8	65.2	69.5	73.9	78.3	82.6	86.9	91.3	95.6	100							
24	20.8	25	29.2	33.3	37.5	41.7	45.8	50	54.2	58.3	62.5	66.7	70.8	75	79.1	83.3	87.5	91.6	95.8	100						
25	20	24	28	32	36	40	44	48	52	56	60	64	68	72	76	80	84	88	92	96	100					
26	19.2	23.1	26.9	30.8	34.6	38.5	42.3	46.2	50	53.8	57.7	61.5	65.4	69.2	73.1	76.9	80.8	84.6	88.5	92.3	96.2	100				
27	18.5	22.2	25.9	29.6	33.3	37	40.7	44.4	48.1	51.9	55.6	59.2	63	66.7	70.4	74.1	77.8	81.5	85.2	88.9	92.6	96.3	100			
28	17.9	21.4	25	28.6	32.1	35.7	39.3	42.9	46.4	50	53.6	57.1	60.7	64.3	67.9	71.4	75	78.6	82.1	85.7	89.3	92.9	96.4	100		
29	17.2	20.7	24.1	27.6	31	34.5	37.9	41.4	44.8	48.3	51.7	55.2	58.6	62.1	65.5	69	72.4	75.9	79.3	82.8	86.2	89.7	93.1	96.6	100	
30	16.7	20	23.3	26.7	30	33.3	36.7	40	43.3	46.7	50	53.3	56.7	60	63.3	66.7	70	73.3	76.7	80	83.3	86.7	90	93.3	96.7	100